My Journey as an Author
(A Memoir)

M. C. Ryder

Copyright © 2024 M. C. Ryder

All rights reserved. No part of this book may be reproduced or transmitted in any form or by any means, electronic or mechanical, including photocopying, recording or by any information storage and retrieval system without permission in writing from the publisher.

M.E.C. Publishing—Lebanon County, PA
ISBN: 979-8-9885074-8-2
eBook ISBN: 979-8-9885074-9-9
Library of Congress Control Number: 2024920822
Title: *My Journey as an Author (A Memoir)*
Author: M. C. Ryder
Digital distribution | 2024
Paperback | 2024

Published in the United States by New Book Authors Publishing

The Dark Series

The Darkest Side of the Moon
A Dance Between Light and Darkness
A Darker Demise (A Compilation of Dark Shorts)
All I See Are Dark Clouds
The Neighbors (A Dark Short)
The Darkened Enchantment
Infinity Tales (A Dark Short)
When Darksome Falls

Non-Fiction Works

How to Stand Up to Bullying
My Journey as an Author

Acknowledgements

As you are about to find out, I've been a writer the majority of my life. My craft wouldn't be what it is today without the support of my teachers and mentors along the way including the ones from my courses with The Institute of Children's Literature. Although my experience took a turn when I had an instructor change, was frustrated when criticized for sometimes the smallest of things, and lost my spark halfway through, I gained valuable knowledge.

I may have taken a backseat for a while to process the tough feedback before I attacked the next story. The publishing world is ever changing, and it's easy to fall behind. The most valuable lesson I learned along the way is; I don't allow anyone else to put pressure on my shoulders. I make my own deadlines. Becoming an author has been a dream come true, but that is only half the battle. My journey as an author is a continuous one. It doesn't stop after publishing one book or ten. There are some highs and many lows.

Over the course of a year of my author journey, depicted in this memoir, I've learned a lifetime of lessons and I'm still learning every day. I'm blessed to have a supportive family. I'm blessed to have supportive friends. I've been blessed to have more support than most in my field. The support has only given me the courage to not give up because I never know who I might touch along the way and inspire. I continue to work hard trying to navigate the publishing world, but the way the game is played is not always the path for me as I never was and never will be one who walks with the crowd. I dare to be unique.

I'd like to take a moment to acknowledge myself. Yes, myself. I write for myself. Express what I need to express. Write what I want to read. For the ones who choose to read what I write, thank you. I hope my writing empowers you and impacts you in a positive way. The best way to express your gratitude, that tips me as an author, is very simple; write a review.

Table of Contents

Acknowledgements..v
Introduction...ix
Chapter One: The Writing Process 1
Chapter Two: The Music 5
Chapter Three: Process to Publication.............................8
Chapter Four: Marketing 11
Chapter Five: My debut, The Darkest Side of the Moon 16
Chapter Six: Self-Doubt...21
Chapter Seven: Community...25
Chapter Eight: Sales...28
Chapter Nine: A Dance Between Light and Darkness ...31
Chapter Ten: A Darker Demise 34
Chapter Eleven: Reviews...37
Chapter Twelve: DE MODE Magazine..........................43
Chapter Thirteen: Covers...46
Chapter Fourteen: Cupboard Maker Books 49
Chapter Fifteen: The Write Stuff Writer's Conference (Greater Lehigh Valley) 53
Chapter Sixteen: Book Signings 58
Chapter Seventeen: Awards...62
Chapter Eighteen: How to Stand Up to Bullying 67
Chapter Nineteen: Chick Lit Café 72
Chapter Twenty: Red Flags 80
Chapter Twenty-One: Literary Titan and Discourse 84
Chapter Twenty-Two: All I See Are Dark Clouds 90
Chapter Twenty-Three: The Neighbors.........................95
Chapter Twenty-Four: Booklife.....................................99
Chapter Twenty-Five: Firebird Book Awards 102
Chapter Twenty-Six: Weight Loss 106
Chapter Twenty-Seven: New Chapter 112

Chapter Twenty-Eight: The Darkened Enchantment....117
Chapter Twenty-Nine: Infinity Tales...........................121
Chapter Thirty: Burnout...123
Chapter Thirty-One: When Darksome Falls 126
Chapter Thirty-Two: The Holy Spirit 130
Chapter Thirty-Three: The Clowder 132
Chapter Thirty-Four: Final Thoughts............................137
Afterword..139
Sneak Peek Feature From: *The Ride of Your Life*.........143
Sneak Peek Feature From: *Heart & Soul Lyrics*...........149
About the Author 154

Introduction

Who am I? I'm no one of importance. Definitely not perfect. Don't have some fancy degree. My flaws only showcase that I am, indeed, human. I've been writing since I was old enough to put pen to paper. An escape, when I didn't have a book in hand. When you are constantly being told that you can't do something and are surrounded by nothing but negativity, you look for a way out. Writing became my outlet. A place I could go to get away from reality.

Writing became my voice and was something I could control. I didn't have to be a successful author in order to write. Didn't have to write in perfect grammar and spelling, but I am still my own worst critic because those judgmental voices are still in my head.

I wrote about what's on my mind. What I wanted to get out. What I wasn't reading. Sometimes it was easy. Sometimes it was hard. Creativity comes at random times. For me, usually the worst of times. I curse the lights when I beg them to change to red and they don't comply. Annoyed when I would go for a walk to clear my head and that's when the best ideas or lines come. Sometimes I have my phone and other times I don't. There is no on/off switch. I try to visualize one in the back of my mind, but it never works, as the wheels are always turning. A simple picture or song sparks constant ideas. I just don't always have the motivation or time to follow them all through. There's always a story wanting to be told, but some just aren't loud enough.

I am just simply me. My mission is to craft stories that are a blend of what *you,* the readers, want as well as what *I* want, fresh and sincere, that also leaves a lasting impact. I dare to be unique. Dare to bend the rules. I'm also an avid reader and

I'm tired of being let down by the same recycled plots and themes. Tired of nonsense from well named authors who have lost their spark. That just put words on paper and push them out for the sake of their publishers. That uses the same methods over and over again that it becomes dry. The difference between a well-written story and a story that's vague are the characters themselves. If you can visualize a clear picture of that character and feel what they feel, smell what they smell, see what they see, fear what they fear, then that is character depth. Character development is like peeling an onion, layer by layer, until you get to the core. If you lose direction of who that character is, then they have not been developed properly. The writer lost sight of their character.

One thing for certain, traditional publishing was something that I always knew wasn't for me. I don't write on anyone else's deadlines but my own. My dream was always to one day become an author. To share my stories. I just didn't know how to make it possible when there were so many rules and biases from "the experts." I knew what was right for me. I just didn't know how to go about it. Knew if I was going to publish something, I wanted to have a say in every step of the way. All my life, I've had doors slammed in my face, just like everyone else. After a while, you stop trying and don't even bother. That's what they want. The experts think they know what works and what doesn't, don't like to go outside of the norm. Don't want a failure on their resume. They forget who they were before they became what they are now. There are no rewards without risks. How many famous authors went through the same cycle of rejection before hard work and dedication in believing in themselves and their work paid off? There are quite a few that come to mind. Just because they got rejected, didn't make them quit. If you believe in something wholeheartedly, then you are already successful.

It's okay to make mistakes. I know for certain I have made many along the way, but you know what; it's how we learn and grow. Making a mistake is not the end of the world. I've made plenty and will continue to as I navigate this wild ride into the publishing world. It's also a way of life. Don't let anyone make you feel like a small mistake, that does no harm, is detrimental. It's only harmful if you repeat it and then it's deliberate. The only thing in your control is to distance yourself from the negative.

Everything changed in August 2022. I didn't set my hopes too high because I didn't want to be left with another disappointment. I sent in my manuscript and within two hours received an email. When I first came across New Book Authors Publishing, I thought it was too good to be true. Looked for red flags, but couldn't find any. Not even my gut was telling me to back out. In the world we live in, you always have to be on guard. There is always someone who preys on the innocent. What I found really interesting was the fact that they had a page dedicated to identifying publishing scams. Who does that? In this world, everyone is out for themselves. All anyone cares about is making a buck no matter what they have to do to get it. New Book Authors Publishing was the opposite. Their fee is pretty reasonable and affordable. Now there are extra services that can be added on that make the price tag go up, but if you can manage to afford it, it's definitely an option to consider, especially if you are a first-time author. The other thing that sold me was owning the full rights to my craft. That was a major deal to me.

I'm a fan of paperback. Not so much hardback. I will wait for a new book, even by one of my favorite authors, to be released on paperback, so my collection is the same size. What I don't like about the industry is how long they drag it out before they release them on paperback. I know they do it on purpose to make people cave, so they can get more money spent on hardbacks. It's ridiculous, especially when there used to be a certain amount of time that I could count on before the paperbacks were released and then they would push back the dates. When it comes to paperback releases,

I'm a troll. Paperbacks are more reasonably priced and are easier to manage before turning out the lights at night.

I have mixed feelings on eBooks. Although it helps to reduce the use of paper, I don't want to stare at a screen any more than I have to, especially when I work a full-time job that requires the use of a computer. Plus, I write on my own computer. I don't write with pen and paper as much anymore to be more environmentally friendly. Also, it's easier to rewrite rather than erase and scribble.

I'm conflicted about audible. Know it's the way of the future, but I like hearing a character's voice in my own head and not having it spoiled by someone else reading it. I tried to listen to a free narrative on YouTube once, but it lost my attention. Not only do I like to read at my leisure, but I also read to learn. I pay attention to the little details. If a question pops up when I'm writing, I'll go to one of my several books hanging out on a shelf and page through until I find the answer I'm looking for. In this dog-eat-dog world, it's hard to ask a question that you have no idea what to question in the first place.

Social media is just noise. Sometimes good, but mostly bad. Don't believe everything you read. Don't be influenced by the words of someone spouting off. You're just feeding their appetite.

If there is one thing you should know about me, it's this. I know who I am and who I'm not. Know what I want. Never was and never will be one that follows the crowd. I make my own waves. Take me as I am. I have nothing to prove to anyone, only to myself.

If you want something bad enough, you'll put in the effort. Nothing, and I mean *nothing* in this life, comes for free. You have to earn it every step of the way.

Chapter One
The Writing Process

I have been a writer my whole life through trial and error. I would watch television shows or read a book and get frustrated how predictable they were. Craved characters I could relate to which were rare gems to find. Since they weren't out there to find, I would write them myself.

Humans are complex characters to write. When I was young, most of my stories included animals, mostly wolves. I found it easier to write from a wolf's perspective rather than a human's perspective. Ironic, since I'm human. When I did write stories with a human as the main character, I got frustrated and didn't finish. Dialogue is by far the hardest to write for a character because it has to be their voice, not mine. It's hard to try to think how a character would react or speak when I don't know them. I just know their outer shell. A wolf character or animal character was much easier because of body language or vocal sounds. I've been around cats my whole life and picked up practically every wolf book out there, mostly for the pictures. I had plenty of references.

A character isn't real to me until they have a name. They are just a distorted picture in the back of my mind. Naming characters is a process all in itself and very important to me. I don't just pick random names I have a ton of baby books and search for baby names online. The name has to have some kind of meaning that fits with the character I'm brainstorming for the story. I will go through hundreds of names until I find the one. And that is just for the main character. I also have to consider every other potential character that relates to the story. And then if another character would need introduced, that will slow me down as I take a break and search for the right one. The side characters don't take as long, but I have to like the name and it can't be something I've used in the past.

Once I have my names, I'm ready to begin. After writing *The Darkest Side of the Moon,* the process finally clicked what I had to do. The process did not work skipping ahead and writing the middle and end before the beginning. When I went back to the beginning, things I ended up writing didn't fit with what I wrote ahead. I had to change a lot, and it got frustrating, which is why it took me over ten years to write. When I finally did finish it, I learned not to skip ahead. I needed to pace myself. Even though I knew what I wanted to have happen at the end, I had to be patient.

Going into *A Dance Between Light and Darkness*, I did just that, paced myself. In my mind, I always knew the storyline was going to be a trilogy. How I was going to get there was another thing. I just went with the flow. I had the fantasy world created, so all I had to do was expand upon it. The second story was an opportunity to really dive into how the vampires worked in my world. I was learning about my own world as I was writing it. Introduced more characters than I intended, but they all worked and fit in the story. Describing what they all looked like was a challenge. I don't like to make them too similar. Again, good old Google is a resource. Shapes of faces, eyes, body types. Even random pictures of people online. I will say, my least favorite part. It's another thing that slows me down as I take time to research it.

Research. Good old research. I am not an expert at all in a lot of things I write about. The one good thing about technology this day and age is, there are a lot of resources out there by people who like to post about it. I filter through many articles and YouTube videos, picking out the similarities and molding it into my story.

Google Maps and Zillow are the best resources for someone like me who doesn't travel much. I can picture a place in my head, but it's overwhelming to broaden the area. That is where they both come into play. I will look for property available online that is similar to what I have pictured in my mind. Sometimes it does change when I find something in a good location, like the blue house in *The Darkest Side of the Moon*. I get to see pictures of the property both inside and outside on Zillow to be able to describe the place, but also make it my own based on my character's needs. Get to widen the map on Google Maps and find other places I can tie into my story. I will admit, some of those places are on my bucket list to travel to.

Once I have the names, descriptions, and locations mapped out, it's time to actually write the story. The fuzzy image of the character is not a character, but an actual person now. And they have a story that wants to be heard. I'm always thinking ahead and jutting down ideas along the way, but I don't stress about it until I get to that point. I do some of the necessary research ahead of time, however I don't do anything with it until I reach that point in the story. Learned that researching when writing the scenes at the time is better for me than doing all the research in advance.

There are many informative YouTube channels out there that tell you to outline your story in advance. I found that does not work for me at all. I've done that in the past. You know what happened? I checked out of the story. There was no need to write it anymore when I knew what was going to happen at what point. Grew frustrated when I had to go back to the beginning when I was already mentally at the end. Writing takes you into a place far back in your mind. Everything else around you, reality wise, takes a back seat. I am physically and mentally there with my characters every step of the way. Music helps to get me there as well. The zone, if you want to call it something. Once I'm there, magic happens. You don't really know what's inside of you until you just let it free. Often times, I think to myself, where did that come from? I wrote that? I can't believe I wrote something that powerful.

My Journey as an Author

It takes a lot of energy to find the right words to express the images I see in my mind's eye. No one, unless you are a writer, will ever understand that. Words are more than just words. The wrong ones can be used to cut people down. The right ones can be used to empower. If only more people used the right ones instead of the wrong ones.

Chapter Two
The Music

Music is everything to me. Showcases how others feel exactly what I feel. That I'm not alone in this big wide world. Allows me to sing at the top of my lungs exactly what I feel inside. In the car, of course, or in the house. Never in public. Takes me to a place away from reality, even if it's only for three minutes. It's enough to boost my mood. I listen to a variety of music.

I don't recall the first book I read that listed a playlist of music the author listened to while writing. Thought that was a neat idea to include. Helps to get the reader in the zone the author went through when writing. Showcases the tone of certain scenes. Stayed in the back of my mind.

I started brainstorming *The Darkest Side of the Moon* after I had a dream that stuck with me for many years and still to this day. Along the way, daily life helped influence the story arc. Music was another heavy influence. Particularly Within Temptation's album *The Unforgiving*. I've heard many artists describe their albums as narrating a story from the first song to the last song. To me, I could never visualize a story in my head. Some songs were completely different in tone and style and just didn't pull me in to see or hear what they wanted me to. And that's okay. I know I'm different. Everyone is. Everyone experiences something in a unique way. There is absolutely nothing wrong with the way someone experiences something for the first time.

The Unforgiving was the first album ever that I could visualize a story from the first song to the last song. There's even a comic book that ties in with the album. I've looked at

My Journey as an Author

the images online, but I did not get the comic because I liked the story in my mind and I didn't want it to be tarnished. It was the album that drove me to go back to *The Darkest Side of the Moon* and try to finish it. The only problem was, I still had the beginning to finish, whereas the music helped drive the ending. When I did finally reach the ending, you better believe that the whole album was playing the entire time.

I have a thirst for music that speaks to me. Radio is background noise that overplays catchy music that the industry wants to shove down our throats. Not all of it is terrible music, but when you hear the same song repeatedly, it gets annoying when there is so much music out there that gets overlooked. I get it; I do. It's what sells and what's new and popular. Sometimes I do enjoy a song being repeated over and over again, like *Perfect* by Ed Sheeran. I got so good at predicting what time of day, three times, when it would be played and at generally what time when I was at work listening to the radio all day long. That time in my life is a story in itself. Maybe one day it will be written. Word of advice, never scorn a writer. Shout out to the team at Elvis Duran and the Morning Show for helping me through a rough time even though they had no idea.

Inspiration comes when you least expect it. Often at the wrong times. Too many songs are feel good songs that convey what you feel. I feel it too, but I can also get lost in them. As I mentioned earlier, it's all about the right words and the meaning they hold. My favorite songs are the ones that are impactful. That gets you thinking.

When I hit a wall while writing *A Dance Between Light and Darkness*, it was Natalie Taylor's song *Love Is The Answer* that helped me finish writing the story. That planted the seed what the series was all about in the first place. When I went back and reread *The Darkest Side of the Moon*, it was there the whole time, I just didn't make the connection. I've heard so many songs about love, sappy ones are not my favorite. It really depends on my mood though. Sometimes I can dislike a song and then later I make the connection the words are trying to convey and then it becomes my favorite song. Sometimes the opposite. I can love a song and then get sick of it. If I choose to overplay it, that is my prerogative.

Music is powerful and brings us all together. It doesn't matter who you are. We all have the same emotions. We all have struggles. It is music that helps take us away from our problems, even if it's only for three minutes. In those three minutes, we are free. Truly free from judgements and prejudice.

Chapter Three
Process to Publication

Even though I received an email within two hours from New Book Authors Publishing expressing their interest in working with me, I was still hesitant. I asked a lot of questions before I agreed to work with them. There are a lot of independent authors, also known as indie authors, who do much of the work themselves. There's writing the story of course, formatting the document, creating a book cover, editing (everyone's favorite), buying ISBN numbers, and a lot of other little details that the team at New Book Authors Publishing did for me in which I am grateful. It was a lot to process, but they made everything as smooth sailing as possible. Publishing a book is not as easy as 1, 2, 3. There are a lot of little details to take into consideration and I'm glad I had their support and still do.

Once everything was completed, or so I thought, my book went live to all the major retailers online with IngramSpark. I was so excited to pull up my book on Amazon, Barnes and Noble, Books-A-Million, and other retailers I never heard of before. I was the first in line to buy my own book. My mother was second. I was so eager to get my book to market that I missed catching a major detail. I approved my book cover, and it wasn't until I had the actual book in hand that it was caught. My mother was actually the one to point it out. A simple word missed on the spine. *Moon.*

I emailed my team at once. I was embarrassed. Couldn't believe I missed that detail. That was a process itself. I also took the opportunity to re-edit my debut novel because now that I had the physical copy in my hand, a lot more issues jumped out at me. Reading something over and over again on a screen becomes redundant. Also, when printing on paper, certain things aren't placed where you want them.

My debut went down for about two weeks until I was able to make the revisions with my team. About seventy copies or more were printed and shipped out before revised. No idea how many were actually printed with Amazon, as every now and then when I bought from Amazon it was still the bad copy. Most were bought by family and friends, but if you are still with me and reading this and happen to have one of those amateur copies, I do apologize, but thank you for not giving up on me. Like I mentioned earlier, I'm not perfect. I am human.

Building up a platform is not an easy task, especially when you are starting from the ground up. I'm not big on social media. Back in the day, I had Myspace. The first of many social media outlets. Then moved onto Facebook. Had Twitter for a brief shining moment, but couldn't stand the character limit, so deactivated it. I mean, hello, I am a writer! Don't limit me!

It got tiresome trying to keep up with all the new social media platforms. I decided, for myself, that I didn't need an account on every single one. Like I mentioned earlier, it's just a lot of noise. I wasn't going to get sucked into that. Don't need the added stress. Don't want to be glued to technology. It's like trying to be a "cool kid" at the table. You will do anything to get noticed.

With my debut novel being released, I had to make some changes. I am a visual person, but don't have the time to commit to a YouTube channel. I know that may hurt me since that's where a lot of my targeted audience hangs out, according to other Young Adult (YA) authors out there, but I'm okay with it because my novels aren't just for young adults. They are for everyone.

Even though I didn't enjoy Twitter when I used it for personal use, it was the perfect social media outlet for my author presence. I didn't want to make another Facebook account, but I did start one only to back out. Later on, when I was trying to get set up with Goodreads, I found out that they didn't have enough information to verify I was who I said I was. The easiest solution was to set up a Facebook account. From there, I set up a Facebook page for my author name. I also ended up setting up an Instagram account. One of the best decisions I made. It allowed me the visualize element after all.

Goodreads. When it first came onto my radar, I checked it out back in the day, but it didn't hook me in. Now as a published author, it's a good resource, that's free to utilize. It was a process itself, though. My book didn't just magically appear in their system. I had to create a form to the Goodreads Librarians Group and request my book to be added to their system. I spent a while through the FAQ page figuring out how that process worked. Once I followed the steps, in a matter of a couple of days, my book was added. From there, I was able to claim my profile page and receive my official author badge, after trial and error, of course.

The last thing on my list was my official author website. I am not a professional and I still worked a full-time job. I now understand why other authors quit their day job to become full-time writers because, yeah, it's a full-time job. To me, it's a side job. My hobby, but it still involves a lot of work. A lot of *hard* work. Lucky for me, I made an investment and purchased the extra marketing through New Book Authors Publishing, which included assistance on building up my website.

Thank God I did, because that was a stressful time. I tend to be stubborn. I like to do things for myself and have a hard time asking for help. Only this was beyond my expertise. I didn't have the time to dedicate into trying to figure it out. I tried. Really, I did, but I was so lost. This was something I needed to watch in order to understand and I didn't want to mess anything up. So, I swallowed my pride and phoned my friend. Em did an amazing job on it. There wasn't too much I needed to adjust. Now all I had to do was figure out how to update it for future needs. That's something I could take my time on, which I did and was able to figure it out, thankfully. Now it's fun!

Chapter Four
Marketing

Like a lot of new authors, publishing a novel was my first goal and longtime dream. I still had work to do. Actually, the work had just begun. Writing is easy for me, well, when I make time. Going through the process to get my written stories published into a novel wasn't so bad. Especially when I had all the power. I made all the decisions. Some, I was certain for my first time. In a world where there is always someone over my head, I couldn't fathom that I was the one in full control. That I was the CEO of my own business. Once I made the connection, the sky was the limit. All my life I held back because I thought my ideas weren't good enough or they got turned down. After a while, I just stopped giving my opinions.

It hurt when I pitched an idea and was told no, only for my idea to be utilized and given credit to another. We've all been there. I wasn't going to be treated that way in the publishing world. I knew for certain traditional publishing was not my path. I just had to wait a while for the right way for me. Independent publishing is daunting. There's too many out there trying to trick you for a buck. Too many dishonest predators preying on the inexperience. If something sounds too good to be true, it usually is.

So, when I stumbled upon New Book Authors Publishing website, I read every word on every page including the part about publishing scams. I may be a novice, but I'm not naïve. I know how to spot a scam and they executed it perfectly. They gained some of my trust by being forthcoming. What publishing company gives free advice like that? Only one who is serious about helping serious writers achieve their lifelong passion; to become an author.

I took a chance. Submitted my first story and left it up to fate. Either it was meant to be or it wasn't. If they didn't like what I pitched, I wasn't going to be let down. I wasn't expecting anything except, to be honest, a no. I was shocked when I received a response within two hours. The ball got rolling and before I knew it my first book was available for sale. Did I have a few hiccups along the way? Of course, I did. Every newbie does. It was a learning experience. They are wonderful to work with. I know they are extremely busy, but they treated me as if I was their top priority. Every email that I sent, a response was shortly to follow.

Once my book was out there, it was enough for me. I knew about it, but the world did not. I received advice on steps to take to get my book noticed. Some weren't ideal. I was surprised how book reviews are a big deal. How outrageous some places are in receiving a book review that isn't even guaranteed to be positive. I knew my debut wasn't perfect. That there were still editing issues. No way was I going to spend hundreds of dollars for a review that was most likely going to get me a bad review. I would save up for the story that mattered to me the most.

There are a few places that offer free reviews. For my debut, that was the path I decided to take. I did invest in the New Book Authors Publishing marketing package. Got my book on their sister page. Was included in their press release. I wasn't expecting a lot of sales. I thought during the holidays that would push some sales, but nothing. I was a little disappointed with that, but the package offered other advantages that were beneficial to me. Like helping me get my author website up. To me, that was worth the expense as it was just another stressful thing on my plate.

The other online steps I took were creating a Twitter page, creating a Goodreads page, setting up my author profile with Amazon, and eventually creating a Facebook page. I'm not one who likes to be glued to the computer day and night. Yet, here I was glued anyway. It was a process getting it all set up, but once it was, it was easy sailing after.

After those few social media accounts were set up, I was mentally done. One day I was working my full-time job, and the idea came to place quotes on pictures that I take when out on nature walks. I had a recent fascination with taking pictures in inverse on my BlackBerry phone. I never had interest in Instagram because I'm not one who likes to take pictures of myself, but I realized I didn't have to put pictures of myself on Instagram. Once the idea materialized, I was eager to get everything set up. Found some perfect pictures, and the rest is history. Now it's my favorite place to go.

I took the steps, for me, to establish a presence online, but I am not a social queen. I had to think outside of the box. My mission was to put my book in as many hands as I could. When Em, from New Book Authors Publishing, advised me to buy my book from each retailer versus buying directly from the distributor, I was floored that other authors didn't already do that. I mean, I was excited! My story was in book form! Of course, I was going to buy a copy. Several in fact. It was getting close to the holidays, so it was the perfect opportunity to gift my book to my friends and family. The best method for me to get my book into hands is to physically do it myself. Even to people I see on a daily basis at places I go around my home turf.

The funny thing is, a lot of the people I know were overjoyed at knowing someone who authored a book. There was no doubt in my mind one day I was going to get a book published. Excited when I did. It was astounding how happy I made people in my community for an achievement I always set my mind on. That in itself was rewarding. I did my job already. Put smiles on faces. I never set out to be the next J. K. Rowling. Frankly, don't want that popularity, but I do want people to read my stories. So, I had to think outside of the box. My favorite place is a bookstore. They are too few and far in between. Not only did I want my book published, I wanted to be able to one day walk into a bookstore and see it

My Journey as an Author

on a shelf. The only way to do that is to request it to be added. Even though it gives me anxiety just thinking about it, I know as an author I would need to also do book signings. Some days I am brave and some days I am cocooned inside. One thing about achieving my dream is it brought me closer to distant relatives. Closer to some friends. It made me realize I am not as alone as I thought I once was.

Libraries were another hidden gem. I hadn't been to a library since I was a child. Stopped going when I was old enough to make my own money and buy the books I wanted to read. Even if they do pile up. I also like reading at my leisure. Don't like being rushed or told what to read. It depends on my mood, what I decide to pick up and dedicate my time to. I also wanted my book available in my community, so I donated copies around the whole county.

The internet is a nice place for some free publicity, but not everyone pays attention. You can't reach everyone who might be interested, plus in one eye and out the next if it doesn't make them stop to pay attention. I'm not made of money. I had to think of a way to leave something behind that people could keep. What's a book without a bookmark? I don't need to pay money to have them crafted when I can make them myself. They don't need to be fancy. Just enough information to advertise my book that people can keep. A keepsake. Trial and error lead me to make one with enough room to sign it. What's even more special about a bookmark? Knowing one is handmade by the actual author and is signed. And it's FREE.

I'm a little shy. Not one who likes the spotlight. I like to go to places and leave my bookmarks behind for anyone who wants to take them. Who doesn't like free? I went to a restaurant with a friend and left a bookmark along with a tip. Normally, I would bounce out as soon as I paid, but my friend paid with a card not cash, like I did. When the waiter came back, he had the bookmark and asked which one of us was M. C. Ryder. I pleaded the fifth.

Told him about my book. He was a nice guy. Told me it was a great idea placing my bookmark with the payment and tip. Thought at first it was a Christian pamphlet. We shared a laugh. It was something different and I think I made his night. He seemed interested. I intrigued him for sure. Gave me a confidence boost. Once I open up, I can be a talker. Just need an icebreaker. Even if he doesn't buy my book, that's okay. He has something to always remember me by and can maybe help spread the word. One thing I know for certain, I made his night a bit brighter, and I left with contentment.

Now, every time I go out to eat, knowing it doesn't upset the waitresses or waiters, I leave a bookmark with the tip.

Chapter Five
My debut, The Darkest Side of the Moon

The one that started it all. My debut. I can still remember the dream lingering clearly. Standing in a cabin. Facing two guys. Their faces were vague, but having a sense of security with them present. Waking up wanting to go back and finish the dream. To understand it. Why was I in the cabin? Who were the two guys? So many unanswered questions. One of many dreams I've recalled. I believe I wrote it down somewhere. One of many that sparked a story idea.

The Darkest Side of the Moon did not come easy. The dream planted the seed, but I did not have a clear direction. The *Twilight* saga helped sprout that seed, especially when I heard that Stephenie Meyer got the idea from her own dream. My story started to develop in my mind, but when it came down to sitting and writing it, I drew a blank. Knew I wanted to make it my own. I plotted out how it would end. Focused on Nadine and Marc's relationship, knowing it would turn into a romance. Skipped ahead and wrote the scene that was playing in my mind because I grew impatient with the progress.

Big mistake.

I've written many stories before, beginning to end. Jotted down scenes that came to mind to save for later when the time came. Sometimes those scenes fit into the story, other times it ended up not fitting.

I learned a valuable lesson choosing to jump ahead. It didn't work! At least not for me. Writing characters is a learning process. You know the exterior of the character, but as you write them, you peel back layers of them along the way and things change. Who your character was in the beginning is not necessarily who they are by the end. They change and evolve. Grow and develop. Become stronger and wiser. Find out what they are made of.

The Darkest Side of the Moon took me over a decade to complete. It is not without flaws. I know that more than any critic out there because I am my own worst critic. There are parts that I could have written better. Scenes that could have been stronger. I got frustrated though and wanted to move on. Don't get me wrong, I love this story and without it, the rest of the series would have never been born. This one started it all. And I am proud how it turned out.

I first wrote the story in third-person narrative, but I wasn't happy with the tone. One day I performed a search. I've always written in first-person or third-person narrative, but never second-person narrative. Decided, why not? Why not change it to second-person and see what happens? That was a daunting task. Basically, rewriting the whole story, again. The last thing I wanted to do. However, I continued to change the sound and the story blossomed. I liked the idea that I was making *you,* the reader, the character. I've read a lot of books in my lifetime, but I can't recall a single one that was in second-person narrative. I was taking a huge risk. Especially for my debut.

Leo, the orange tabby, was always a character in my novel. My whole life I've always lived with a cat. It was just normal to have him as a side character. When my best friend, Tiggie, passed away, I wanted to honor him. I had Tiggie for a short period of time. Five years. Those five years seemed a lifetime. Taking him in when he was in need of a home wasn't easy. I already had two other cats and I knew one was going to be a problem. I hate when I'm right, but I was willing to do whatever it took to let Tiggie live out the rest of his golden years. He deserved a loving home with a family, not a shelter.

Tiggie came into my life just when I hit a wall of uncertainty. I appreciated him being there for me and making me laugh. He was both independent and craved closeness. We had a strong bond. Greeted me as soon as I walked in the door. He loved his nightly lunchmeat. Considered everything a toy. Loved to rip up mail. Invited himself to help play Monopoly. Had a nightly ritual of giving me his kitty massages, I referred to them as. How I miss them and waking up to him beside me, even if he did hog the bed.

Tiggie was a special kitty. I incorporated parts of him into Leo, but Leo is still his own character. Tiggie lives on in Leo, always. I'm broken by how things ended so badly for Tiggie. I knew there was something wrong. He acted different. Took him to the vet, twice, but they couldn't find anything. Came home and found him highly upset because he made a mess on himself. Cleaned him up, but he was still in distress. Hid under my bed and started panting, heavily, which cats just don't do. He cried and cried. I didn't know what was wrong. Didn't know what to do for him since it was late at night and the vet was closed. It was clear he was suffering. He also acted like he had to go to the bathroom, so I picked him up and tried to help him. He ended up biting down on my thumb, hard.

He didn't have to go to the bathroom. He was just in extreme discomfort. I took care of my thumb and called the emergency line to the vet. Took him in. Decided the best thing for him was to have him cross the rainbow bridge. He was eighteen, even though he didn't act his age. Thought he had many more years in him.

The worst part was feeling like I failed him. Since he bit my thumb, the vet had to report it. The bite was bad enough that I had to go to the ER. By law, they had to verify he didn't have rabies. I hate that they had to cut him up just to confirm what I already knew. He didn't have rabies.

Before he took his last breath, I spoke in his ear that I knew he didn't mean to bite me. I knew it was out of fear and pain. He never hurt me like that deliberately. When I annoyed him, he would whack his sharp claws at me, but he never once bit me. Not like that.

I had tickets to a Skillet concert. I've always wanted to go see them, but after the ordeal, I just couldn't drag myself out to see them when I was sad. It's still hard to listen to their song, *Anchor*, without tears flooding my eyes.

So, yes, Leo is a tribute to my best friend Tiggie who will forever live on. There was only one way to do that, to have Leo become a vampire cat. It never crossed my mind when I started writing *The Darkest Side of the Moon*, but we all have Tiggie to thank. He made an impact in my life and an impact in my stories.

There's a quote by Mark Twain, "Write what you know." What I know best is myself. There are elements of me in each of my main female characters. One thing I share with Nadine is my love of cinnamon. Little did I know my preferred spice would have a bigger impact in a later story, after some research.

I don't know about other authors, but I will admit that Marc is my favorite character. Team Marc! I try not to be biased, however, in every story I write, I'm always surprised by which character tends to steal my heart. Marc actually wasn't a surprise and yet, when I wrote his own short story, it made me adore him even more.

Reading is my favorite pastime, but I've grown tired of the predictable and copied storylines. I like different. Like stories with meaningful purpose and symbolism. Enjoy rare gems. The stories I want to read are hard to find, especially with all the noise in our society telling us what to read. After writing my own, it's even harder. My mission has always been to write captivating stories that make you keep turning the page and take you on a rollercoaster ride of emotion, leaving an impactful lasting impression.

The irony of writing my story is how my own words circled back to me. *Even on the darkest of nights, the sun still rises.* That line stuck with me during my own dark time. Repeated it over and over again, even on those rainy, dreary days. Even my own words speak to me.

My Journey as an Author

How I end my debut was a risky move. Good plot twist at the time, until my mind starting wondering what people would think. I know some won't understand. Some will get mad even. It's okay, I know how to take the heat. What I hope most people take away is this; when someone is forced to be someone they're not, it ends up destroying their well-being.

Chapter Six
Self-Doubt

Just like every other artist in the world, I yo-yoed with self-doubt. Still do. There were days where I believed I would take the world by storm, and then there were days where I just wanted to crawl into a hole and hide. Who was I to think I had what it takes to shine in this big world that's always in competition? I'm no expert. I'm not cut-throat when it comes to selling. If you say no, I won't push.

When my debut was published, I spread the word to friends and family, but I had a small base. Fear twisted me in all kinds of directions, realizing that people I knew would possibly read my words, my story. I'm a private person. Letting someone read my story, even if it's fictional, was personal. You only get to know someone when they choose to peel back layers of themselves. Reading my crafted story was a layer of myself reflected in the characters. Going in, they didn't know that, but I did. I didn't know what they would think. Would they think differently of me? Would I scare some off?

No news is good news, right? Wrong. Silence is an answer in itself too. Sometimes good. Sometimes bad. It was hard to be patient for the people I knew to get back to me. The ones that did had nothing but positive feedback. Going into this business, I mentally prepared for the negative, but didn't get much. At least not to my face.

A negative comment is a reflection of what you already know and reinforces that self-doubt, while a positive comment boosts your spirit and encourages self-esteem. That one positive feedback means the world to anyone who receives it. In this society, there is way too much toxicity that beats people down so far that they don't know how to rise above it all due to envy. It's okay to not like something someone else likes, but it's not okay to berate them.

A kind word or act goes much further than unkindness. Leaves a lasting impression in one's soul. Is the sustenance needed to nourish the mindset that, *I am good enough*. Everyone fights inner battles every day. The voice of reason whispers while the voice of doubt shouts. It's the kindness that helps the voice of reason drown out the voice of doubt.

One of my biggest self-doubts was being my own editor. I utilized my mom as well. The two biggest no-no's that I kept hearing repeated over and over again from everyone. I searched high and low in the beginning for an editor, but never found one that met my terms at an affordable rate. I had the option of purchasing the copyediting package with New Book Authors Publishing, which was better than what I was finding out there, but in order to release multiple books in a course of a year, I had to make cuts. The plus was New Book Authors Publishing also did do a once over when reviewing, so another set of eyes were on my manuscripts and they caught some things that I missed.

I expected some negative feedback with my debut, *The Darkest Side of the Moon,* and even the sequel, *A Dance Between Light and Darkness*. What I did not expect was some bashing with *A Darker Demise*. Like every author goes through, I had hiccups in the beginning and learned from my mistakes, so when it came time to publish *A Darker Demise*, I took all the right steps. Ordered my proof, read through my proof, adjusted some minor details I caught in print form, verified, and published. So, when I got a review back stating I had "many" errors, it hurt. It was like studying hard for my history test in high school and ending up getting a D. I put in the effort and didn't get the result I was hoping for.

After that negative review, I went on the hunt again. Found an editor, Genalea Barker, who checked all my boxes. Was an author herself and recently just published her first novel. I reached out to her for more details and sent the first five pages of the manuscript I was working on getting published. I didn't hear back right away, but let it slide as I had other things on my plate. Received a spam email from her that informed her email was down. Knew exactly how that felt as I was there. I emailed her back and waited some more. Meanwhile, I reached out to my team at New Book Authors Publishing and informed them about hiring an editor. I was concerned they would be offended. Long story short, Em informed me what I really needed to hear. That I was the "best editor of your work" and "one of the best at fine tuning their manuscript." Everyone takes for granted that you know your worth. It's always a warm feeling to know people recognize it even when you question it.

I took the fact that Genalea's email issue was a universal sign that I was not supposed to move forward with her services. She was completely understandable about my decision. Through the process I gained another supporter.

Comparing yourself to others is self-destruction. Just like our fingerprints, we are all unique. It's our differences that guide us to see in a new light, if one has an open mind. I won't lie, I'm guilty of comparing myself to those I admire from afar. Every time I see an error, I realize that they are a flawed human too. Everyone makes mistakes, and it's okay. They don't always need pointed out, but it does boost my self-confidence that even the great ones make mistakes too.

There are always good days and bad days. That will never change. It's a cycle that repeats over and over again. Just when I think I've climbed out; I get pulled back in.

When the sales stopped coming in, the self-doubt was quick to whisper this was the end. I didn't make it. No one wanted to read my story. Still had friends who had yet to read the story or comment if they did. I stopped asking. If they really enjoyed the story, they would have said something. I shouldn't have to push and ask. It's just nice to have someone other than my family to talk to about my story.

My Journey as an Author

I had to remind myself, at that time, that my book was only made available for two months. Two months! Calm down. I'm not going to be an overnight sensation when I'm a nobody and there are thousands of books out there in the sea to read. There are many steps I have to take. Even one of the greats, like J. K. Rowling, didn't become an overnight sensation. It took her four years of hard work to get where she is today!

There's another side to self-doubt, self-worth. I gained so much confidence in myself from the positive feedback that I stopped doubting myself. Instead, it turned into self-worth. I knew in my heart I was worthy, but I started questioning myself. I put a lot of time, funds, and effort into trying to spread the word, my way, however I wasn't getting the results I was hoping. Unless I was paying someone their time to read my book(s), I wasn't really grabbing ahold of reader's attention to invest in my craft. A bit disheartening because I knew they had great messages everyone could benefit from. Even putting a physical copy in people's hands didn't guarantee they would actually read it. Donating copies to the libraries didn't guarantee members would select it, especially since they had no idea a local author's book was added to the collection. One disheartening thing after another.

The major, being underestimated by the "experts." That's where self-worth started creeping in. On my low days, I just wanted to give up. To stop trying. Was disgusted when my eyes were open to how the publishing business worked. But I didn't. I refused to be buried in not belonging without making some kind of noise. The thing I've learned along the way is, when you give up, you fail. Even though there were days where I didn't feel worthy, I didn't allow self-worth to defeat me because I knew in every fiber of my well-being, I'm worthy.

Chapter Seven
Community

When I released my debut, I shared the news with my family, friends, and co-workers. I wasn't really expecting too much. I was excited that I finally achieved my longtime dream. What astonished me was how they all reacted to my accomplishment. They were beyond thrilled to know someone "famous" who wrote a book. I laughed and told them that I'm not famous.

I didn't realize how big of a deal it was to actually publish a book. I mean people publish books every day. I've always been a writer. Now I could refer to myself as an author. I was proud of myself. Proud that I fulfilled my dream. I still had a long road ahead though. Being an author is one thing, but getting people to actually read your book is another. I knew it was going to be hard work to get my book noticed by the right people.

I gave my books out like candy to everyone I knew who was interested in having a copy. I didn't ask for anything back. I was happy to give them, signed. Mailed signed copies to family and friends out of state. Let me tell you, that was a process itself. Trying to remember who I talked to, who I gave copies to, and who I hadn't. And if I forgot anyone, I'm sorry.

I will admit I was also nervous about what my family, friends, and co-workers would think about my story. The beginning, not so much, but the end does get dark. Having strangers read my story wasn't as nerve-racking for me because it's their choice to read if it's something that

My Journey as an Author

interests them in their genre. I got to see a different side of the people I thought I knew.

Even though my book was in people's hands, it was the holidays, so them having time to read my book was another factor. Also, if they were in the middle of reading a book, I know what it's like not to want to read something else before you finish. It was really hard for me to not spoil it for anyone and when someone did finish; I talked for hours about it. I really enjoyed the feedback I got from my cousins because pretty much every reaction I was aiming for, they reacted accordingly. It was nice to have someone else to talk to about my book other than my mom.

The next thing on my bucket list was donating a copy of my book to the local libraries. For a while I put it off. Putting myself out there was daunting. I'm not a good salesperson. I'm not a pushy person. The best path for me was to go to the library. A place I hadn't been in a very long time. Once I started making my own money, I bought the books I wanted. There was a time when I could devour everything I picked out of a library within a certain timeframe, but these days I don't like to be rushed. Sometimes I pick up a book and I don't read it until many years later. It all depends on my mood. What sounded good when I first read the back of the cover now doesn't interest me, especially if it's from an author that I'm not familiar with.

When I finally worked up the nerve to go to the first library, I didn't do so well. I stopped in, gave a little introduction, and handed over my book. Basically, I ran back out. After taking in a couple of deep breaths, I processed everything. The one thing that stood out to me the most was the huge smile on the librarian's face.

As I drove to the next library, I realized a lot of details I lacked to mention. With a deep breath, I entered the second library and remained calm, cool, and collected. The librarians were a delight! Got me talking, and I emerged from my shell. The environment was open, warm, and positive. Once I got started, I was a jabber mouth. I knew from the first librarian that the director had to approve the book and enter it into their system before it would be put on the shelf. The librarian assured me that the director most likely would and that they might make an announcement from there. Music to my ears! Another free way for me to get the word out.

I stopped at several more libraries around the county. I had limited days and times since the libraries closed around the time that I got off of work. I got to meet with one of the directors. She was pleasant and explained the process to me that it could take about a month before my book became available. Bonus, she enjoys reading books in the genre I market in. Met another director who told me based off the blurb on the back of the cover, my book sounded interesting. It's always nice to hear something positive! Even from someone I don't expect it from.

I hit gold. Had to sign up for a library card, but that wasn't a problem for me. In fact, I don't know why I ever stopped going to the library in the first place. Just like most of the world, I kind of forgot they existed. Searching through their websites was an eye opener and fueled many ideas for the future. I realized working with the libraries was going to be very beneficial for me. They host events. Have book clubs. Know people, especially book people. And the most rewarding thing was putting a simple smile on faces. Again, achieving my longtime dream had a way of making others happy. I don't need to be rich and famous; I was already successful.

Chapter Eight
Sales

Just like every new author, I had a period of obsession with checking my sales, every day. It's not a healthy obsession. Don't do it. If you do, you need to get off that wagon as soon as possible. You need to limit yourself. I cut back to once a week. Created a spreadsheet so I could keep track.

Just because I handed out a bookmark or a post was put out didn't mean someone was going to buy my book that same day. When I reevaluated my life and how I buy books, I don't always buy them the moment they are available. Not unless I am eagerly awaiting one from my favorite author and even then, sometimes time gets away from me. When I'm writing, I typically don't read because I don't want to subconsciously write something that I just read.

My first month I sold a decent amount for being a nobody. Now, of course, most of those sales were my own and my mom, but I also had some family and friends buy a copy too. I honestly can't tell you how many were not actually my purchases. I lost track, but once I stopped buying the number pretty much stayed the same. That was when I started to become obsessed. At the end of the year, I told myself no more. I'm going to cut back and go to once a week.

I may not utilize YouTube for my own means, but I am actively watching videos and YouTube stalks me like everyone else. Sometimes it is for my benefit. Just like everything else, I limit myself, but if someone's video catches my eye and tags what is on my mind, I will view it. Some of those videos include other authors out there who express the painstaking process of being an indie author. The one that stood out to me was this guy saying his book only sold two copies. Well, at least I did something right because I sold more than two my first month.

Another YouTube video that I watched mentioned that a typical book by an indie author may only sell a hundred copies in its lifetime. Well, after two months, I was slightly over that so, again, I was doing something right. It did make me wonder, though, are those indie authors putting in the work or giving up too soon? If you want to sell books, you have to put yourself out there even if it is outside of your comfort zone. You can't expect people to line up for your book if they don't even know who you are. You get what you give. And even after a few months when the sales slowdown, what is stopping you from still spreading the word? If the book is still available, start a conversation. Do some research into free marketing opportunities online. Think outside of the box. Never give up.

I thought my book being released around the holidays would have been a good thing, but I believe it only held me back. Everyone was busy and businesses closed early for the holidays, so I wasn't able to get out there on the streets and start spreading the word. Also, people were too busy to read. Sometimes it was hard to be patient. Frustrating when I was eager to know what my friends and co-workers thought. I received a lot of positive feedback from my family, but they're family. I was living in a bubble. All I heard was positive feedback. I'm not naïve though, I knew negative was sure to come. I know how to handle the negative, it's harder for me to handle the positive. I don't know how to act. It's sad really. This world is so full of hate and pessimism that when you receive optimism, you question it.

When I wrote my stories, I always knew I wanted them to be a trilogy. Then I wrote some short stories that tied in. After I finished the process of my debut, my others were pretty much ready. I didn't want to release them too soon, and then one day I decided to add an insert for my short stories into the back of my sequel. After I did that, I decided to add an insert of my third novel, in the series, to the back of my compilation of short stories. Then figured, why not do it for all of them? I've read many books where I saw that marketing strategy. At the time, it was just a way to tease my readers and let them know there is more to come. As I processed it some more, I realized that was a brilliant marketing strategy to help sell future books.

As you might remember, I'm not always good with patience. When I read a book from an author that is set to be a series, I despise waiting a year or more for the next one to come out. Even though I remember the characters and how the book made me feel when lost in that world, I don't remember everything. Unless it's a really good book, I don't read them again because I already devoted my time and I rather devote it to another book. Plus, I already know what happens. There are so many out there that need to be read.

So, yeah, I'm different. I wrote all my stories back-to-back and decided I wanted them out there as soon as possible. Now, I did have a budget and had to be mindful. What I realized by putting an insert of each additional novel I had sitting by waiting to be released was, they will eventually sell themselves. All I have to do is hook some readers interest, doesn't matter when, but when I do, they most likely will want to read the *entire* series. I did something right without even realizing it.

Chapter Nine
A Dance Between Light and Darkness

The Darkest Side of the Moon took me over ten years to write while *A Dance Between Light and Darkness* took me around five months. I took a different approach. I knew I needed to continue Vince's story. Knew I was going to introduce Melia, who was actually featured in the first story, but was an unnamed character. Knew what direction I wanted the story to go, just didn't know how I was going to get there. This time I didn't jump ahead. I took my time and went with the flow.

The first chapter I'm aware I loaded pretty much everything from the first novel. Referred as "info dump." I needed to get it out of my system though. However, when I reread it, it didn't seem as terrible as I originally thought. That's for you to decide, but I was content with how it turned out and could move on.

Melia was the polar opposite of Nadine. This was my opportunity to write the transformation into becoming a vampire in my world so, Melia was the one to do just that. That was fun getting to know how it worked as I wrote chapter by chapter.

I knew the story was as much Vince's side as well as Melia's side of the story. It just made sense to write it in third-person narrative. It started off strong, and it was easy to slip between the two characters because they were of different genders and in different places mentally.

Vince started off in a dark place. Melia was his light at the end of the tunnel. Innocent and pure. When she slipped into a dark place, it was Vince that pulled her back into the light. I enjoyed writing that contrast. The third act was their dance. A metaphor for their feelings they tried suppressing. There was actual dancing too.

By the time I got to the third act, *The Dance*, I was uncertain how to carry the story to the grand finale. I knew the events that were going to happen, I just didn't know how to lead up to it. What the hidden meaning truly was in my story. So, I took a break. Listened to some music on YouTube to spark inspiration. Nothing spoke to me at first until a song popped up titled *Love Is The Answer* by Natalie Taylor. I never heard of her before or listened to anything she sang. I had been intrigued by the title and decided to listen to the song. I'm glad I did. It pulled me in right away and kept my interest. It was a good song. The more I listened to the lyrics, the lightbulb clicked on above my head. My story was more than about light and darkness. It was also about love and hate. In the end, love prevails. Not only was that the hidden theme that really was staring me in the face the whole time, I realized that was the message I was trying to get across in the other stories I wrote. That song allowed me to connect the dots that tied all of my stories together and was the driving point in more to come.

Melia's character was necessary for the story, however, after a while, I grew annoyed with her character. She was too sweet. Too down to earth. Too innocent. Didn't have backbone. Didn't know how to stand up for herself. Was whinny. Like I said, completely opposite of Nadine and for good reasons, but writing it was obnoxious. I have to wonder if any other authors get frustrated with their own characters. This was a first for me.

On a lighter note, Niles was the one that surprised me. My star character. I adored him, just like Melia. He was fun to write. He definitely wins the title of being my favorite. Every scene he appeared, made me laugh. I gave him some good lines.

I also enjoyed writing the alliance between Vince and Lamont. Two alpha males working together in harmony. Setting aside their differences and teaming up. Lamont realized some of his faults and made sure not to repeat them. Knew where Vince came from and still had his back, no matter what. A wise wolf. I love his character growth from *The Darkest Side of the Moon*. It wasn't planned. He was more of a guide for Vince, like Gabriel was for Nadine.

I had some good quotes in my debut novel. I had even more in the sequel. Words can be powerful in the right order. I love what I came up with regarding forgiveness. You hear about it a lot, but actually embracing my character's flaws and learning the meaning of true forgiveness, even if another person does an unspeakable act, really struck a chord. I think I ended up portraying that well. There was a lot of hurt, anger, and resentment in Vince. In order for him to let that go, he had to find a way to forgive. Writing it was a good lesson for myself.

Cecily was another favorite character of mine. The original plan was to write her as someone who was blind, but it didn't work out that way. Instead, I explored a path that was new terrain for me. She was an older character and wise. Finding her voice was challenging. I had wise characters before, so I needed to make her a different kind of wise. Adding new characters is fun, but also challenging. Each character is unique to the story and in order for them not to be confused with other character's speech, they need depth. That depth needs to be believable even if they are just a minor character.

The big bad Maximilian. I like a good villain. I also like leading readers down a certain path and completely twisting things around. It's a lot of fun. One thing I enjoy is a shocking turn of events. I like changing things up. The ancestry aspect was a lot to take in. I spent countless hours mapping it out. Even I was befuddled. It was a lot to take in and get right in writing.

Let me tell you something. You never know who you inspire with your talent. Even if you don't get feedback, inspiring just one person with your gift is all that matters at the end of the day. That's all I strive to do. Being yourself is always good enough. Aspire to inspire.

Chapter Ten
A Darker Demise

A Darker Demise is a compilation of three short stories. The first is *A Unity of Balance,* which is Immilla's story. I tried to avoid creating my own magic system, but that didn't work out. The vampires and werewolves had to come from somewhere. They didn't just evolve out of thin air. I dug deep within myself when writing. Wrote one chapter and then put it aside, uncertain of the direction. Nadine was a heavy influence as she shared the same start of life as Immilla. The setting of the sun with warm, vibrant colors. Fire in the sky.

When I reread the first chapter, it was strong. I was worried I would not be able to deliver a compelling story for Immilla. I just let my mind run free as I focused on her as a character. Little by little, my magic system started to piece together. Even when I completed her journal entries, I was still learning about my own magic system, but I had a better understanding of it. It wasn't until I wrote *All I See Are Dark Clouds* when I completely understood the type of magic I was referencing. Something completely different. When I went back and reread my earlier stories, I was flabbergasted that I didn't see it before.

Writing is like constructing a large puzzle with tiny pieces. You see what the big picture looks like, even if it is blurry, but sometimes it's hard to know where to start. You just got to start fitting pieces and hope for the best. Sometimes, there is no rhyme or reason. You just have to go with the flow and find the right pieces. They won't connect themselves if you just stare. The more you fit, the image starts to become clear.

By the end, it's easier to complete when you finally grasp the bigger picture.

One word defined my magic system.

Devine.

Now when I go back and read Immilla's story, it makes perfect sense. I see it with a new lens. It was there all along. I just didn't have all the right pieces yet. I do have to admit, it's a story that surprised me. At times, it even amazes me that *I* wrote something so powerful and deep. Sometimes it's the shorter stories that have the most impactful meaning.

There are many impactful lines. Maybe one day they will be used as quotes. Looking at a list of ones I have saved, the one that jumps out at me is: *A gift should be shared, not be kept for oneself.*

The next short dark story in *A Darker Demise* is Marc's story, *My Salvation*. Like I mentioned earlier, Marc was my favorite character. It was only right to give him his own story. Got to explore more of his background. It was a great idea until I reached the end. What was I thinking rewriting such a heart-wrenching scene not once, but twice? It was definitely harder the second time around. It actually made me sick to my stomach. I've seen memes on social media questioning if authors get affected by certain scenes in their stories. I can't speak for all authors, but I can speak for myself. Yes!

What I loved about Nadine's character was her sass. What I enjoyed with Marc was him giving it right back to her. Getting to rewrite those scenes from his perspective was thoroughly amusing. Just like you, the readers, I got to learn more about Marc in writing his story. Made me fall in love with him even more.

The last dark story in *A Darker Demise* is a Nadine short, *The Path to Redemption*. I was eager to write in second-person narrative again and utilized the concept, *what if?* I knew the end game, but I didn't know the journey she would have to embark on first. It was a path that I don't think has ever been questioned before. At least not that I know of. I

My Journey as an Author

had to dig deep again. Embark on the journey with her. I like what I accomplished in each of my short stories. In writing them, they opened my eyes to a few things. Always there in the back of my mind, but now surfaced to the forefront. I can only hope that I've awakened you along the way too.

All three are strong in their own sense, but Nadine's short is one I'm proud of the most. I still pinch myself in disbelief that I was able to craft something to that magnitude. If there is one story that everyone in the world should read, I think that one is it.

Chapter Eleven
Reviews

When my debut was published, I received a list of places I could get professional reviews. I hit up the ones that were free. Looked into the others that costed money. It ranged from $50 to over $400. I'm not made of money. I have limits. I'm not one who likes to gamble. There is no guarantee if I spend over $400 on a review that it was going to be a positive one.

To me it just wasn't worth it at the time. It was a game I had no interest in playing. Yes, it's nice to flash a review in your book or on your website from a respectable and well-known reviewer, but I just couldn't bring myself to do it. At least not when it came to my debut, as I knew it wasn't flawless. I tend to skip those plastered reviews in books. I don't read something because there's a $400 review telling me to. I read it because it captures my interest.

Yes, I'm aware there are benefits in receiving flashy and expensive reviews. Getting more promotion. I wanted to attract the right readers, not the wrong ones. Word of mouth spreads just as fast, like wildfire, by the right people. I don't need to become a best-selling author. That wasn't my dream. My dream was to become an author, and I accomplished that. However, I realized that was actually the wrong mindset to have, as reviews are a way to build up your book's resume. So, I kept the costly reviews in the back of my mind, especially for one particular story I was passionate about when the time came when it was published. Sometimes, in order to make money, you have to spend money. I wasn't confident I would receive a good costly review with my first two novels, as I had a different frame of mind when writing them, but *All I See Are Dark Clouds* was another matter. I was willing to take a big risk with that story. That's when the fire in my fingers really took off.

There is a term called beta readers. I searched how to find some, but I wasn't fond of the idea of releasing my manuscript to a bunch of strangers before it was published, especially when it's hard these days to tell who are legitimate and who are scammers. I rather send my formatted manuscript after it's published for feedback. A risky move, I know. However, they're my stories and at this point nothing is going to get changed, only possibly enhanced in the future. I already knew how to do that. It's been done before with my debut. Besides, any minor detail in any of my stories would have a negative impact on the other ones. Minor details are everything.

There are a few YouTube channels I watch regularly. Some fellow indie authors I follow who have found success their own way. Some of them even helped inspire me to get back in the writing saddle. Provided encouraging words at the right time when I needed it the most. I figured why not reach out to them? I poured out my heart and soul when sending a message. Not one who typically reaches out. I watch from afar. I may not have taken the right approach at the time, as I never heard back from them. I won't lie. I was disappointed. Mentally came up with every excuse I could think imaginable as to why I didn't hear anything back until I stopped. Silence is an answer in itself. Speaks volumes. I could read the writing on the wall. I wasn't going to dwell in my disappointment, just move on. In the end, it's them who lost out on an opportunity because I always have ideas that they could have also benefited. I will pay it forward to those who help me along the way, when I'm a nobody, but I owe you nothing if you don't even acknowledge me. If you treat me as an individual before I make something of myself, I usually remember that. I'm like an elephant, I don't forget an act of kindness and I'm pretty good at sniffing out when it's fake.

In this business, you have to learn what benefits you and how to be firm. Not everyone has your best interest at heart. Now that I was put in the position of being the CEO of my own business, I wasn't going to allow anyone to run over me. "No" must be in your vocabulary or you will get run over. Let me tell you something, I'm not afraid to say no. In fact, it's wonderful to be able to give those a taste of their own medicine.

I'm not a pushy person. If you tell me no, I move on. Simple as that. In the back of my mind all I can think is, it's your loss, not mine. I will pitch ideas. Either someone likes them or they don't. I'll find another way because I have ambition and I'm not afraid to walk alone. In fact, I'm used to it.

Everyone will want to be your best friend, for a price, if they can make money off of you. They will sweet talk to you dripping with honey, feeding you exactly what you want to hear to hook you in before dropping the price bomb. Don't be too eager to agree to anything. Tell them you will consider their offer and research everything you can about them and their company. Some have good intentions, most don't. I listen to what my inner voice tells me. The first approach by someone I don't know, especially via the Internet, speaks volumes. If there is a negative projection, I'll test the waters, but I won't bite. Sometimes, though, it benefits me into building up followers. It takes just one person of importance to take notice. One to start a chain reaction.

After a period of nothing, I caved and spent funds on a review for my debut *The Darkest Side of the Moon* with Readers' Favorite. Since it was over 90 days, I got a discount for a two-week express review, the cheapest. I was pleased with my review, especially the part that indicated it was a "page-turner," exactly what I was going for and now it was in black and white. I figured out how to add the review on my Amazon author page. A moment where I felt like a

My Journey as an Author

professional author. It's really the little things that mean everything.

My views on the expensive reviews shifted once I hit a wall. Every year my mom asks me what I want for my birthday or Christmas. It's the same answer every time, I don't know. I have what I want, material-wise, and if I don't, I purchase it myself with my own money. It's true that money can't buy happiness. Only a dose. Now, I had an answer I could give her. Reviews! A good investment that could only help me reach more readers.

I don't recall when I stumbled onto Chick Lit Café. Good old Google stalking me is what led me to them. I reviewed their website and was impressed especially since there was a book featured on their website which was the talk of the publishing world at the time. I figured, why not? Why not try to reach out to them? I had nothing to lose. My only reservation was the price tag, since it wasn't listed anywhere. I suspected it would be way over my budget. In less than twenty-four hours, I heard back from them. They were impressed with my cover, read the sample, and loved that it was written in second-person narrative. They wanted to start the process immediately, and the plan I selected was in my budget. I'm still in disbelief that me, an independent author doing all of the work myself, managed to achieve something that was going to open a lot more doors for me. I mean the books featured on their website were from big name authors and trending books. A pinch me moment. It was like I won the lottery.

While my book was under review with Chick Lit Café, I had other reviewers I met on Instagram post their review on their socials and blog. A short time after their posts, I received a message from DE MODE Magazine. I never heard of the magazine, but something whispered in the back of my mind not to dismiss them. I'm glad I listened to that inner voice and reached out for some feedback.

Waiting patiently is the hardest thing to do. I entered my books into other book award contests however, results wouldn't be announced until the end of the year. Following different groups on Facebook led me to Literary Titan. Not only did they offer a book review, but they also automatically entered your book into their book award program. An opportunity to win an award sooner rather than later.

I worked hard building up my resume with my debut, *The Darkest Side of the Moon*, and yet was told by Chick Lit Cafe my reviews on Amazon were low. At the time, I had nine. For an independent author, I thought that was good, plus I had editorial reviews from some respected places in the publishing industry. I went back and asked all my family and friends to post a review which took a week and a half. My concern was Amazon would believe the added reviews were not legit and delete them since they were all getting posted around the same time. After I got my reviews up to fifteen, it still wasn't good enough, as there were only three "verified purchasers." At that time, that was when I had to use "no." I had had enough. I did what was asked of me, but all they saw was an opportunity to make more money off of me from already spending a lot to promote my book they had yet to start when they had it for three months. Let me make something very clear. Every website an author can go to, to get an "honest review" that gets posted on Amazon, or Goodreads, or Barnes and Nobles in which you have to *pay* them to do you a service, in which they state somewhere that you are "not paying for a review," is a lie. You are absolutely paying for their time to read your book in exchange for writing a review. There are no ands, ifs, or buts about it. A monster scam to desperate authors who want their books to become buzzworthy. And I will admit, I got pulled into that vortex of lies and it brought my positive outlook down to a negative mindset. What an author is really paying for is, a way to get ahead into the publishing industry in order to see their books flash as one of the top books to read on mainstream sites. You must remind yourself every day, who's your targeted audience and how do you reach them? Reviews are a great way to build your book's resume, but they are not always a reader's deciding factor into investing into an author's work. The cover is the first thing that captures a reader's interest. The back blurb is the second that entices the reader to turn to the first page. The sample they are allowed to review is the third act to get the reader hooked. And the fourth, reading over reviews. How do I know this? I'm also an avid reader. Those are always the steps I take. I read reviews between the lines. Ignore the five-star reviews, because come on, I'm not naïve those are the ones that are usually "paid" for. I read the one-star reviews with a grain of salt because those are just individuals who want their fifteen minutes of fame. My focus are all the ones in between. Those are usually the more authentic ones from actual readers. I don't like taking one individual's opinion at face value to make a decision for myself. Most of the time the books that many despise are the hidden gems while the ones that are "loved" are really a load of crap and teaches toxic mindsets.

There was a point in which I became so low in disgust I lost sight of the point in why I wanted to become an author in the first place. I steered into the wrong lane and found it hard to reroute. Being able to voice my frustration in a safe place was the charge I needed. The fire rekindled. If there's one thing I refuse, it's admitting to defeat. It's easy to do and that much harder to rise stronger from the ashes.

An accomplishment I managed and proud of is the day, Labor Day 2023, in fact, when I found out I received a 5-star review with Readers' Favorite for *All I See Are Dark Clouds*. I knew my prior works weren't perfect, so when I got 4-star reviews, I wasn't blindsided. I put in more effort, learning from my mistakes, and thrilled my hard work finally merited the 5-star status. A few days later, *The Neighbors* also achieved a 5-star review with Readers' Favorite. Delighted that a second-person narrative work of fiction achieved that status. Again, I put in the extra hard work to get it in tip top shape, editing wise, and my hard work had paid off.

Chapter Twelve
DE MODE Magazine

When DE MODE Magazine reached out to me, I was in a low place. My grandmother had just passed away five days prior. The day before, at my job, I did not expect to have no one say one word to me as if nothing happened, but radio silence is what I got. Ironic how I was dreading going into the office, not really wanting to talk about what I went through, but having no one say a word was worse.

There were a few people at the office that knew some of what I was going through with my grandmother, just no one in my department. The thing is, when I called off "sick" the Friday after my grandmother passed, I reported exactly why I was calling off. So, to be met with radio silence was appalling.

There are things that I'll take to the grave. Back in August, when I submitted *The Darkest Side of the Moon,* was when my grandmother was first admitted to the hospital. She was never an easy person to live with, and was in and out of the hospital for a couple of months. I mentally prepared for the end, but it didn't come at that time. Instead, she got sent home to die. It was not easy to work from home, take care of her, take care of the house, take care of the cats, and still try to finish The Dark series while watching someone slowly deteriorate. I really don't know how I did it, but when you have no other choice, you just do it. Things got so bad that I unintentionally starved myself.

The world preaches about asking for help, but when you do, you don't get the kind you truly need. Exactly why I never liked asking for help. Exactly why I take on everything myself even though I am only one person, but I refuse to depend on others. They almost always fail me in the end. My biggest fear was that my grandmother would die when I was alone with her. That's exactly what happened, only I wasn't afraid when it did happen. I was relieved.

She put my mom and I threw a lot of torment because she wasn't getting what she wanted. You can make an excuse that it was dementia. You can make an excuse that there was a demon inside of her. I lived with her my entire life. I knew exactly what it was that she wanted. There's no doubt in my mind she had some dementia, but towards the end, she was more herself than when she went into the hospital. She was a stubborn woman. So was I. I repeatedly played Pink's song "Just Say I'm Sorry," over and over to her again. In the afternoon, while working from home, she fell. I got her up and to the bathroom where she broke down and apologized to me for everything that she ever did to me and asked for forgiveness. I accepted and forgave her. It's all I ever wanted. Never thought I would get it.

After work, I spent time with her. While she was sleeping, I made supper. She woke as I was finishing dinner and I gave her a plate. She asked for help to the bathroom. Was unsteady on her feet and nearly fell even with her walker. I helped her to the bathroom, but was at a disadvantage since the walker was between her and me as she backed into the bathroom. She fell off the toilet. I got her back on the toilet and cleaned the floor. Stepped away for a few seconds to get a hold of my mom, who was at work, when I heard a thump. She fell face first onto the floor and was gone. Just like that. The thing is, I know that she found peace.

Even though the image was still raw, when DE MODE Magazine reached out, I couldn't help sense there was a reason they discovered me. I never heard of them and my first thought was to dismiss them, but something in the back of my mind kept telling me not to say no outright.

I reached out to my team at New Book Authors Publishing and Lacy, who I met in a Facebook group. They agreed that it looked promising and didn't see any red flags. So, I responded and completed the information required. Some of the interview questions were challenging, but it was the first time I had an opportunity to answer some interview questions. I was not fond of having to submit a picture of myself. I'm camera shy, but if I was going to have a picture taken of myself, I wanted to do it right. So, I went to Cupboard Maker Books for my unprofessional photo shot. I wanted to include Cupboard Maker Books name, but there was too much background and too little of me. I love butterflies, so it was fitting for me to stand at the second popular place in the bookstore for a photo.

It was a victory when it was published and another milestone achievement in my author journey, plus they're very supportive of me on my socials with many of my posts.

Chapter Thirteen
Covers

One of the main reasons I went with New Book Authors Publishing was the fact that they had the resources I didn't in crafting a book cover for my novels. That process was something I had no idea where to begin. I know there are resources out there, but I didn't have the patience to figure it out. I already knew in my mind what I wanted, I just needed help to find the right images.

The cover for *The Darkest Side of the Moon* wasn't exactly what I had pictured, but I also didn't know how it would look if the image in my mind was selected. What I had in mind was a new moon with a sliver ring glow surrounding the moon, but then the cover would have been too dark. I also knew I wanted an image of the Dragon's Eye symbol somewhere on the cover, but I didn't want it to take away from the cover either.

When I was sent a few options for the cover, the only one I liked was the one that ended up becoming the cover. As soon as I saw it, it spoke to me. I didn't want a full moon. However, the contrast of the image was exactly what the book represented. Black and white. Yin and Yang. Light and darkness. I also loved the reflection of the moon in the water, so I gave my approval. After trial and error, the Dragon's Eye symbol ended up on the spine. I didn't want it to take away from the cover and didn't think it would look right on the back cover. The spine was perfect and I decided to keep up with that theme for my future novels. A symbol on the spine.

I went in knowing everything was not going to end up the way I envisioned. There are times you do have to give a little. The cover was one of those things. If I had gone the traditional road, I would have had even less input. The thing is, it's still a good cover. It still draws you in. That's exactly what I wanted.

For *A Dance Between Light and Darkness*, I knew I wanted fire on the cover. Different colors of fire. Orange and blue. I knew what I wanted and conveyed my idea to the team. Since I was very detailed about it, they sent me the website that they select the cover images from. The sky was the limit once I got my hands on it! I searched through hundreds of images of fire. Nothing really popped out at me, but I selected the few that were satisfactory and passed them along for feedback. I also looked up cover images for *A Darker Demise,* at the same time, which was much easier since I knew I wanted foggy woods. Found one within no time.

I ended up going back and forth with Em regarding the cover for *A Dance Between Light and Darkness*. She had her concerns about the ones I picked out and provided alternatives. I wasn't a fan of the ones she picked out either. There were a few that were promising, but none of them jumped out at me. I had voiced I wanted a spiral symbol on the cover and Em came up with the idea of a spiral fire on the cover. I liked the idea immediately and was mentally smacking myself over the head, wondering why I hadn't thought of that. See, sometimes two heads are better than one! So, I did more digging and I still wasn't finding the one. Changed my wording around because on the internet, wording is everything.

You have to find the right words in order to get the right results. Somewhere along the way, there were images referencing fire and ice and again I was smacking myself. I love that representation. In my mind, that always represented Nadine and Vince. Within Temptation even has a song about it! One of the ones I love the most on the album, *The*

Unforgiving. So, with the right wording, I finally found the cover art for *A Dance Between Light and Darkness,* and Alyssa worked her magic. I was over the moon, yeah pun kind of intended ha-ha. It wasn't what I had envisioned, it was better! I couldn't wait to get a physical copy in my hand! For me, I hit another milestone. A beautiful book cover and one that I was able to pick out from a sea of thousands of images.

Now that I had the website where the team utilized cover art from, I was a girl on a mission. You see, I had all my other stories already written and had an idea of what I wanted for each cover. Had it all outlined. So, with a Monkey, my cat, sleeping on my lap, I dived in and found cover after cover for all my future novels.

After the ordeal with *A Dance Between Light and Darkness*, I went back and performed different searches for *The Darkened Enchantment*. What I envisioned was something I knew wasn't going to happen unless I created it myself or teamed up with an artist. That was something I was putting off for the future since it wasn't on my doorstep yet, however I went back and reworded what I wanted. I knew I wanted an image of a dragon tree. They were all images in daylight. I would have liked the image of the tree to appear how Cleo drew it, but that was not something I was looking forward to when the time came. When I went back to search images of the tree, I searched "dark dragon tree." There were not many images available at nighttime of the tree, but there was one that I saw that I knew was the one instantly. Let my mom take a look at it along with the other three that popped up and she agreed that it was the standout one. Appropriate because there were stars in the night sky and it followed the first two covers. A dark theme.

The problem with working ahead and finding covers you love is the waiting game. It took every ounce of my willpower, and funds, of course, not to just release every single novel at the same time. Sometimes it's hard to hold back and pace yourself.

Chapter Fourteen
Cupboard Maker Books

I went to visit a friend where she worked at The Outlet Shoppes of Gettysburg and delivered a signed copy of my debut. While I was there, I saw there was a bookstore. Book Warehouse. I was excited! First, it's a bookstore! Where I live, bookstores do not exist anymore. The only bookstores are the giant chains and even they are a distance away. And second, it was an opportunity, my first, to try to sell myself as a new author.

This was before I went to the libraries. I shopped around and had to work up the nerve before I took the plunge. With a deep breath, I made my entrance. Asked to speak with the manager, which so happened to be the lady who greeted me upon entry. I introduced myself and she told me congratulations. She was so easy to talk to.

I was discouraged to find out that the store was closing after Christmas though. She was very upset about it and the daunting task of trying to find a new job afterwards. I knew how she felt. I was there once. It's an overwhelming experience, the unknown, but sometimes you are meant to go through a dark time in order to get to where you are meant to be. I told her as such to try to help her with the transition. Spoke as many words of encouragement as I could. She did give me advice though. Two things that stuck with me from that visit was that writing is considered a craft, and the other was the owner at Cupboard Maker Books in Enola. Not only does she work with other authors, but there are also cats roaming in the store. My dream bookstore! The only thing missing is coffee.

My Journey as an Author

I left with a bunch of books that day and even though I don't remember the manager's name, I'm ashamed to admit, I still think about her and I hope the best for her. Hope that some of my words spoke to her or even my story. The one good thing she said was at least she had something to read.

I didn't travel to Cupboard Maker Books right away. Kept it in the back of my mind. I did look at their website and liked what I saw. I knew eventually I would pay a visit. Sometimes I have to work up the nerve to travel to places I've never been to before, driving wise. I could only do so much in one day and I had just gone to Gettysburg. The drive was actually easier than I had anticipated. I always expect the worst.

The next thing on my agenda was donating a copy of my books to the local libraries now that the holidays were over. I had off work on Martin Luther King Jr. day, the irony, and stopped at the Hershey Public Library. The process of donating my book was a little different from what I had become used to. Had to fill out a form for my novel to be included in the Local Authors Shelf collection. I also learned the library hosts the Chocolate Town Book Festival, which, again, I'm ashamed to admit, I've never heard of until I donated my book. Can you tell I'm not generally a social person? When there are crowds, I'm not usually there. I did agree to partake in the festival when the time came.

While I was at the Hershey Public Library, I was referred again to Cupboard Maker Books. Since I had the day off and I had one book left, I decided to make my way out there. First, I had to pick up my GPS. A wonderful device that gives me confidence to drive into unknown territory. Of course, because I'm stubborn and had a hidden agenda on the way back, I went the more difficult route that led me into the city of Harrisburg. Maybe one day I will update my GPS. That day was not that day. It's okay, my phone is backup.

When I got to Cupboard Maker Books, I did a little browsing before I introduced myself to Michelle, the owner. Right away, I received nothing but positive vibes. I knew this was the place that I was meant to be, that was going to help me achieve my long-term dream as an author. Before I stepped into her bookstore, I approached a manager at one of the Barnes and Nobles, but I didn't get positive vibes from the interaction. I was kind of disappointed. Publishing a book was my first dream. Seeing it in a bookstore was my second. I was mentally preparing to see that dream not come true, but I wasn't going to give up on the fight. I was going to allow it to happen naturally, hopefully.

There's a saying along the lines of "being at the right place at the right time." That was so true on Martin Luther King Jr. day. As it so happened, Michelle was offering a free author class and encouraged me to attend that following weekend. It took me some time to find it on her website, but I did and I attended. Learned a lot in her course of two hours. Learned exactly why I had bad vibes from the manager at Barnes and Noble. My eyes were opened. Granted, if I'm invited for a book signing, I will absolutely attend, but I will be providing my own books. It's the business side that scared me the most. It's new terrain. The team at New Book Authors Publishing are a good resource to have and I can ask as many questions that I have, but it's always better to have someone with whom you can speak to face to face.

When I attended the author class at Cupboard Maker Books, Michelle mentioned she was interviewing us while also informing us on how the business side works. Funny, because I was also interviewing her. She's also the very first person that I got to meet, that also wrote a book. So, she knows firsthand what it takes. I had a mentor to go to.

I picked up a copy of her debut that night and read it. It's a very good read. The main character is relatable. I love a good mystery. I recommend it. *Death of a Saleswoman A Death Motors Mystery.* Kept my interest the entire time. Not going to lie, after writing my stories, I found it hard to find good reads afterwards.

I returned with more questions about how the book signing process worked. Michelle encouraged me to come out during a specific time to meet a fellow author and get a feel. I met a new friend that evening and gained more confidence, as I had my first book signing in the works with Cupboard Maker Books.

Chapter Fifteen
The Write Stuff Writer's Conference (Greater Lehigh Valley)

There's a writer's conference retreat in Virginia that I've been eyeing up for the last several years that I've been wanting to attend, but it's for a week. As a cat mom, with needy furry children, it's hard for me to get away for long periods of time. Before them, I had older needy cats that needed to be separated because they didn't get along in the same space. A story for another time.

So, since the week-long writer's conference was not an option, I performed a search for other conferences that might be close to home, and low and behold, I found a winner. Only three days. Something I could manage to pull off, and it wasn't too far from home. It just so happened to feature Maria V. Snyder as a guest presenter. A name I heard a lot from Michelle when I attended the free author class. There's even a page dedicated to Maria V. Snyder on the Cupboard Maker Books website.

I looked into Maria V. Snyder. Found she authored several books which all but one was a series. At the time, I was not at a place where I could dedicate time to read a series. I don't like to read when I'm writing to avoid incorporating, without realizing it, what I might have just read. The only novel that was a standalone was *Storm Watcher*. I could have ordered the book online, but it gave me a reason to pay Michelle a visit at Cupboard Maker Books. Now that I knew her store existed, I wanted to support my somewhat local bookstore. Plus, I wanted to get the feel of an easier route to travel that was way better than going through the city.

My Journey as an Author

Turns out, I made Michelle's day as her son was behind the drawings in the novel, and she expressed how it would make Maria V. Snyder's day as well, since the novel is near and dear to her heart. As soon as I read the back cover, I knew it was a novel that I was going to enjoy. I love dogs. I love storms. I love any story that incorporates search and rescue. I wrote one myself back in the day, but I don't know if it will ever make it into the publishing world.

Another interesting find on Maria V. Snyder was the fact that she used to be a meteorologist. I love the movie *Twister*. Love chasing storms as a hobby. The irony of how Maria V. Snyder discovered after going to college that it wasn't everything she wanted and more. So, she changed careers. That was always something I never wanted to do. Go to college and end up going down a path completely opposite. I've seen so many people do exactly that. It's what I conveyed in *The Darkest Side of the Moon* that Nadine struggled with. How are you supposed to know what you want to do with the rest of your life at a young age when you are barely an adult? I'm still trying to figure it out.

Once arrangements were made, I signed up for the writing conference and booked a room at the hotel. I had a sense I was meant to be there. It was the right time in my journey that it presented itself. Too many coincidences that I couldn't ignore and consider them a coincidence.

Turns out it was the best decision I ever made for my author career, as I met a great group of both non-professional and professional individuals who share the same passion of writing. Not only did I make new friends, but I learned even professionals, like Maria V. Snyder, who has been in the business for several years, still stumbles over words at times. That was one of my biggest fears, stuttering, as I had agreed to speak at my local libraries. Public speaking is something I generally avoid, but it's part of the author's role. Attending the conference reinforced that I don't have to be perfect. In fact, I know I'm far from it and that's okay.

M. C. Ryder

One aspect I picked up on in the group of aspiring writers was, most were missing the mark. Authors do too, even the well-known ones. A well-crafted story is for the readers, not just for oneself. What I want to read, what I crave to read, is originality. Most see something popular on television or read what is trending, which sparks an idea, but really, they're just rewriting someone else's story with different characters and scenes. You can take themes and plot ideas, but make them your own. Dare to be unique. Teach me something through your writing. Leave a lasting impact.

Aspiring writers forget to ask themselves important big questions. Why does the story matter? What are you trying to convey? Question your character's motives every step of the way. You can outline a character all you want with descriptive detail, a start, but until you are actually writing them, you will find there are more questions you didn't think to ask. You know the exterior, but when you stop procrastinating and start writing, that's when you uncover the interior that unravels until you get to the core. Like peeling layers of an onion.

Names are important. Don't just pull them out of a hat. Pick names with hidden, deeper meaning. Sometimes I spend hours searching for the perfect name. Some come easy, others not so much. My characters are not real to me until they have a name.

A take away I took from the conference was having a tagline, basically a catch phrase. I started writing this mini memoir before I attended and realized I already had one without realizing it. When I had Maria V. Snyder sign my copies of her books, I noticed she wrote something different in each one that was true to the book. After processing, I decided going forward, why not sign my books with my tagline? Something easy to remember and everyone can benefit from it. And, my first book signing was only a month away.

When I first arrived I was shy. Sat in a room with complete strangers. I'm not one who starts conversations, but once I'm out of my shell, the sky is the limit. I met a lovely lady, Dot, from North Carolina, who sat at my table. She told me she likes attending the conference every year. Once I opened up, I gave her some of my handmade bookmarks. I wasn't expecting anything, but she told her daughter, who was excited, and wanted to order my first two books that were out, right away. I made her daughter's day, from a hundred miles away. Always such a good feeling!

Everyone is a different critic with an opinion. Some points in the conference I agreed with, others I didn't. Some can be too nit-picky. All writers have a style. Some are better than others. My eyes were opened to the writing style of some well-known authors who got frowned upon. At the end of the day, it's not about the writing style, it's about the magic of a story and how it changes lives. The big question every writer should ask, how can my story inspire? Readers matter most, not paid critics. Readers are forgiving. When I read, I don't look for flaws. I may see them, but if the story manages to hold my attention, as I have a short attention span, I gloss over it. It's the journey a good story takes me on that matters most.

Attending the conference was worth every penny I spent. I highly recommend to new authors and aspiring writers to find a local writing conference to attend. You don't have to go to one and write. Go to meet individuals that will support your writing journey. Another bonus while attending the conference was meeting a lawyer who also happens to write. I was able to ask the lawyer some questions I had on a story I wrote several years ago, but never pursued publishing as I had reservations. The professional lawyer eased my mind. Now, I had the confidence to publish the story in the future, and if for some reason something were to happen, I now know a lawyer.

The lawyer made an announcement about a free writer's conference called Pocono Liars Club. He had me at free. I have a writer friend that I informed in hopes we could go together. She signed up, but unfortunately was unable to make it. Meanwhile, we attended a writing group at a local library, met other writers, and a self-published author, Mira O'Hart. I attended the Pocono Liars Club with Mira, who told me if it hadn't been for me, she would have never gone on her own. I was already inspiring so many people on my journey.

One negative thing I did take away from each of the writing conferences was the fact that I was looked upon as another wannabe author. I had some huge accomplishments, yet I wasn't taken seriously. My goal wasn't to sell myself, just meet like-minded individuals, but it was a little disheartening. After processing, I realized every author out there is fighting to be seen, to be heard, to have their books read. Like a school of fish swimming all together hard to stand out from the rest in the vast ocean. The only way to stand out is to swim in the opposite direction, even if there are sharks. That frustration and some advice from a presenter at the Pocono Liars Club, *aim high*, led me to enter The Pulitzer Prizes Book competition. I had nothing to lose if I didn't win, except $75, but so much to gain if I would happen to win. I wanted to be taken seriously. That was one of my paths. Before readers could even consider reading my books, I had to get the attention from the experts in the industry.

Chapter Sixteen
Book Signings

There were some lows before I got to partake in my very first book signing. I was at a high when the offer was extended to me by Cupboard Maker Books a few months out. My grandmother passed away two and a half weeks before the event and the week before, I fought tooth and nail not to get sick. I wanted it so bad. Pumped myself with Airborne at the beginning stages and other remedies that I found worked for me. I was successful in chasing away whatever tried to grab a hold of me.

I struggled with the idea of dressing up as my main character, Nadine, from *The Darkest Side of the Moon*. That had always been the plan, but I started to have doubts. Thought about not doing it at all. I also dragged my feet on setting up the prize wheel I had ordered months in advance as well. Lucky for me, it was easy to set up when I opened the box the day before. I'm so glad I didn't back out with my initial plans.

When the day finally arrived, it was a breath of fresh air. I arrived early and was greeted by a good friend of mine and her small children. I was so happy to see them. She surprised me as she kept it under wraps. Her daughter had a grand old time exploring the bookstore and interacting with the store cats. She was also the first one to test out my wheel of fun. She received many prizes.

While I set up my table, another familiar face came out to support me, that I worked with at another job, once upon a time. I was happy to see him and met his wife. Social media has nothing on interacting with someone face to face. Not only did he come out to support me, but he also supported the other authors who were there that day.

One thing I observed during my time slot was how customers steered away from the action. Not only was it intimidating for me to interact with strangers, but it's also intimidating for them too. I thought my prize wheel would help break through that barrier, but it didn't have quite the result I was hoping for. It worked like a charm for the younger folks, however, there weren't as many that came out during my signing.

There was this one young girl I will always remember who wasn't someone I knew. I lured her over with my prize wheel, of course, and then talked up my books. As soon as I mentioned my debut, *The Darkest Side of the Moon*, was written in second-person narrative, she lit up like the fourth of July. She was so excited, jumping up and down saying how cool that was. I made her day and she made my day by making her day. She took off and spoke with her mother, who came over and read the book blurb and they purchased a copy. Just putting a smile on someone's face is so rewarding and bonus I sold a copy!

After my first book signing in May, I had in talks with the owners to do one at Ancestor Coffeehouse and Crêperie. I wanted to hold off until *All I See Are Dark Clouds* was published to do a sort of release party. However, the process delayed longer than I anticipated. Meanwhile, they acquired Swatara Coffee Company. By the time the process got rolling for me, it was mid-July. I made the ultimate decision not to move forward with the book signing with them at the time, as they were busy and I was recovering financially. In order to have book signing events, you need books. I, the author, was responsible with providing those books. Yes, potentially I would make some money at the book signing event, but the stock I had I wanted to keep for my book signing in October that was already locked in.

Even though it was hard to essentially be rejected by the Barnes and Noble manager of the one I sought first, there was a reason for it. At the time, the rejection stung because I realized someone else didn't believe in what I believed in, my craft. It also stung when I received no response from the independent bookstores I reached out to. That was the kind of negative I wasn't expecting, especially when I saw online other independent authors reaching out to their local bookstores, and receiving such positive feedback from doing it. It hurt a lot. What's the point of publishing a book if you can't get a bookstore to feature it? I wasn't expecting hundreds of copies to be added to the store. Just a few. As an avid reader, sometimes you go to the bookstore not knowing what you want, because you're not following the latest trend, and look for whatever catches your interest. I can't catch a potential reader's interest if my book isn't on a shelf for display.

While at my local library's writer's group, I met a guy, Tom, who used to run a comic bookstore and also happened to know Ralph, the owner of Comics & Paperbacks Plus. I grew up in the town the store is located in and went there all the time as a kid to get, you guessed it, books. I went and introduced myself since Ralph expressed interest in meeting me, to Tom. It was a step into the past. The store is exactly the same with minor differences. After a lovely chat, I was able to give a copy of each of my books for him to add, and post about on social media. That boosted my spirits before my book signing in October.

The big day finally arrived. It was a rainy morning and the night before I was scrambling to get everything packed up. I procrastinated in investing in a cash free option and after talking with some local business owners, I decided to go with Square. Tested it out beforehand and was amazed how easy it was to use, like I was told. Until you actually take the dive and get your hands wet, your mind, at least mine, just spins with so many questions. I like mentally being prepared before diving right in. Most of the time I'm thinking afterwards, why was I was so stressed out? You just have to do it. Even if it scares you. Just do it.

M. C. Ryder

I arrived early to the Hershey Library for the Chocolate Town Book Festival. I was placed in the second group to arrive, so watched as the first group arrived and unloaded. When my time slot arrived, I unloaded and found out what table number I was placed, 37.

I went in and was overwhelmed at the number of other authors setting up. Knew there was roughly 50 authors signed up for the event, but the room was jam packed as I navigated the floor looking for my table number. I discovered I was not in the room, but outside in the main part of the library which I was thankful for as it was warm with all the body heat.

When I found my table, I set up right away. My friend surprised me again by showing up with her two children. With new books out she purchased the ones she didn't have and I could test out my Square device, even though I drove to the library a couple days before and tested it out. I still couldn't believe it was that easy.

I had a blast. Although I knew I wouldn't sell as many books as I hoped, due to so many other authors at the event, it was fun to make the young children's day, who were bored while their author parents tried selling books. This one young girl kept coming back to spin my wheel of fun. I figured there was something she wanted she wasn't landing on. Near the end of the event, she finally landed on the candle prize. I was astonished she had not landed on that prize as that was a popular prize so many were landing on.

There was another young girl who was going around asking each author to sign a page in this picture book she had and to write a favorite quote. She also asked for a picture which I was delighted to take. I'm a no one, but to be someone another person wants to take a picture with is a special, warm feeling to experience.

Chapter Seventeen
Awards

Everyone can relate that when they do something that goes above and beyond, they like to be rewarded for it. Some expect more than what they are entitled to, which unfortunately ruins it for others. A smile is a reward in itself, but it's also nice to actually hear praise. However, too many assume nothing positive needs to be said. Positive words and vibes I experienced helped build my confidence when I just wanted to stay retreated in a shell when all I expected was the negative.

I also value having some kind of memento in hand, knowing others recognize my hard work, which is one of the reasons I submitted my stories into the Best Indie Book Awards (BIBA) contest. Was one of the first things I did once I got *The Darkest Side of the Moon* published. I searched for all the literary award contests out there that I was eligible for. Was selective too. What set BIBA apart was the fact the winners receive a trophy. I also wanted to make sure I didn't have to travel because I'm unable to go long distances for a long period of time. It was a win-win for me. I knew I was going to enter all of my stories I published into the contest with the hopes of at least win one. Just one win was satisfactory to me. Just one little trophy to cherish, that I was recognized as being a good talent to some experts.

What astonished me in my research was how not many authors realize winning an award is a good marketing tool. To me, it was a no brainer. I see the seals on books all the time. Always knew I wanted to have that satisfaction that it was a worthy read, even if I don't always agree. It's just a normal thing to me. That's when readers start to take notice; when buzz is created from respectable places.

For months I toyed with wondering if I should enter other award contests. Just because I was entering five different works into different categories didn't mean I was going to win any of them. But what if I did? What if I entered other award contests and won them too? Would that be frowned upon? I was new to the business and didn't know what would be taboo. I honestly didn't know what to expect other than the worst; I wouldn't win. If I didn't win, then I would potentially miss on other opportunities if I held back. Something I'm good at. I sought my mom's advice, and she's my mom and told me to just do it, but again, she's my mom and can be a little biased. I wasn't looking for permission, I was looking for a solid answer. One she really couldn't give. I knew I could have reached out to my team, but I also didn't want to come across as being someone who was greedy. Then one day it hit me. Musicians often win multiple different awards that we watch on television each year and often times sweep multiple categories. What was the difference in the publishing world if I ended up winning multiple awards for my novels? There was no difference. It was another way to grow my platform.

So, with that in mind, I entered other literary award contests. I was still selective. I wasn't looking for a cash reward, even though my mom said I was being foolish in that mindset. Money wasn't what I was after though. I just wanted to know I did a job well done worthy enough to be recognized and hopefully be able to hold a trophy in my hand that I could treasure.

The only problem was the waiting game. I entered the contests early, which some offered a lower fee. Again, I was selective, as there were certain details offered that if I won, I didn't want. For example, Readers' Favorite Book Award Contest offered a chance to be published by a traditional publisher as well as a chance for the winning book to be made into a movie or TV show. Two things I didn't want. I'm ambitious, but not that ambitious. Don't want to sell my rights and don't want my stories to be tarnished in order to be put onto a big screen. Was never my goal.

Like I mentioned once or twice before, I'm not made of money. I was spending more than I was making back in book sales. Had to cut myself off while waiting for my team to work on *All I See Are Dark Clouds* and *The Neighbors*. Knew I would be spending a lot when they were published and had debt to pay off before that time came. I was getting book reviewers off of Instagram and promoting too, but it was costing me money. I was also waiting for Chick Lit Café to complete their review and start promoting as well as waiting for the article to be published in DE MODE Magazine. So, I caved. Entered my first two novels into BookLife for a chance to win $5,000 or even $1,000. A mistake. It was a greedy move and the first true negative feedback I received that was contradicting. A tell sign that I was not taken seriously as an author to my craft. To readers, awards don't mean too much other than seeing a fancy emblem or wording that brags which might catch their eye, but to the literary world, it generates attention. You won't win anything if you don't take a risk. Eventually, something had to pan out to bring in some revenue to help pay back what I was spending. No risk, no reward. I just took the wrong risk. Lost sight of the audience I was trying to reach out to.

After those decisions, DE MODE Magazine published their latest edition, in which I was featured and Literary Titan announced their June 2023 book award winners. There were two reasons why I decided to work with Literary Titan. First, to gain another book review, and second, to potentially win an award for one of my books sooner rather than later. I entered all three of my published works at the same time and when they announced their winners, I was flabbergasted to receive an award for *all* three of my books! It didn't even hit me until Em emailed me that now I could consider myself an award-winning author. My first big milestone in the literary world.

I entered other book award competitions in which the announcements wouldn't be announced until the end of 2023, which included American Book Fest. The winners and finalists were announced a bit earlier than expected and at first, I didn't think I placed at all for any of my books I entered, but then I noticed *A Darker Demise* was listed as a finalist in anthologies. It was another win even if it wasn't first place. Another opportunity to get my author name out there.

When the Best Indie Book Award (BIBA) for 2023 were announced early, I was eager to see if any of my books placed only to be disappointed that none of my books gained a winning status. Ironic that after entering my books I debated about entering other contests. I'm so glad I overcame that hurdle as I would have missed out on opportunities early on. Sometimes the wins you want the most don't always pan out like you hope. In the publishing business, there are always rejections. You can either wallow or let it fuel your fire to be determined to prove those rejections wrong. I'm still determined to get one win in the future with BIBA.

Another book award I entered was the Firebird Book Awards. What I like the most about the awards, which is different from other awards, is the fact the entry fee gives back to those in need. A win-win. I was also presently surprised when all my books placed. Another bonus was the fact that I could participate in an on-air interview. It was an opportunity not to miss out on even though I was extremely nervous, but Pat Rullo had a way to make me feel like I was talking to a friend.

The last 2023 award announcement came from Story Monsters Book Awards. The Royal Dragonfly winners were supposed to be announced by the end of November 2023, however with so many entries, the winners were not announced until the end of December 2023. I might have not won 1st place or 2nd place, but I did get Honorable Mentions for all of my books! A win is still a win, no matter how small. With another win under my belt, I could feature my wins in the New Year edition of Story Monsters Ink magazine which aims as a literary resource for librarians, teachers, and parents. An opportunity not to miss since that's exactly the audience my series aims for.

Chapter Eighteen
How to Stand Up to Bullying

While I was in the midst of publishing *All I See Are Dark Clouds* and *The Neighbors*, I started my first self-help project. Writing an inspirational self-help book was never something I saw myself doing in my lifetime. Sure, I incorporated valuable information in all of my fictional novels, if one pays close attention, and even write lyrics that help get things off my mind. However, I reached a breaking point and poured all of my frustrations into the thing I knew was best for me, writing. When you are constantly surrounded by bullying, even if it's not directed at you, you just reach a point where you can't take it anymore. Writing has always been my healthy outlet. Now that I was finding my voice, I felt it appropriate to do something about it even if I couldn't stand up to the bullies myself face to face.

Sitting out on the sidelines is the hardest thing to do as you listen to friends and family breakdown as to the way they are treated at home or in the workplace. The best thing that I can do is to give them the tools that I've learned over the years, but they have to be brave enough to utilize them. It's not always easy when you are alone. Can't rely on others to fight your battles because you will never learn and grow. I always offer a helping hand and support, but in the end, in order for the nonsense to stop, they have to stand up for themselves. That is the only way to truly stop a bully in their tracks.

Writing it was one thing, but getting it to publication wasn't an easy road. I came across a lot of red tape. In the beginning, I incorporated some resources to reference, only to showcase that I actually knew what I was talking about, even though I had no credentials to back me up. I was a no name trying to make my mark in the world. Reaching out and asking permission is a daunting task. Something I never would have had the courage to do before I started my author journey, but the confidence I gained along the way and how I changed as a person during my dark time outweighed the fear. Plus, the subject matter was something I was extremely passionate about. I had a duty to everyone out there who experiences bullying to publish something that could be beneficial to them.

When I received a decline, it stung. Put a break in my heart, but I didn't let it drown me. I considered it a sign. A sign I was supposed to move forward and eliminate all resources. I didn't need to refer to an expert about proven facts. I lived and breathed bullying day and night. I'm proof that you don't have to resort to a bully's level. That you can break the chains of that mindset.

In order for readers to read and believe in what I was writing about, I had to give examples. Some that were personal and involved my family. It brought some hard conversations in revealing the truth in how I felt about certain situations. Truth that I buried for a long time and only ever got out in writing that was unheard, until now. It was an eye opener. That is what going to therapy is all about. A safe space to open up about how one truly feels, having an intermediate that stops the fingers pointing when others take offense, and to ask those difficult questions one typically avoids. My therapy has always been writing. Now that I was finding my voice, I wasn't shy in backing down anymore as deep wounds were starting to heal.

During my second visit with the writing group at the library, I brought along the first chapter and read it out loud. It was the first time I was brave enough to read something that had yet to be published. I literally had jaws dropped when I concluded. Opened up for the first time my experience, with a group of still kind of strangers, along with my ordeal with my grandma, which had not been intended. It felt so good to release that pain that I had buried within. It so happened that that Friday ended on a holiday weekend and I had to fight tooth and nail to get a few hours off from work, so I could even go. When you want something bad enough, you will fight for it.

The book cover I picked out ended up not being the one that made it to print. I was a little disappointed that it didn't work out as it set a strong message, but the one Em found instead conveyed just as strong a message, and I do believe more eye attracting to not only adolescences, but hopefully adults as well.

I submitted the manuscript after submitting *All I See Are Dark Clouds* and *The Neighbors* in which it ended up being ready for publication before them. I also put a deadline on it as I had looked into submitting it to The Pulitzer Prize in which the deadline was July 14, 2023 and my debut, *The Darkest Side of the Moon,* was not eligible. I had the intention of submitting *All I See Are Dark Clouds*, but with problems getting the cover just right, I knew I was going to miss it. Again, I considered it a universal sign and even though *All I See Are Dark Clouds* is near and dear to my heart, I realized it wasn't appropriate for that kind of honor. Even after submitting *How to Stand Up to Bullying,* I questioned what I was doing. What was I really trying to prove? Here's the honest truth, I just wanted a way to get some recognition as a serious author. To be seen. To be heard. To be loved. What it might cost me, I didn't know. Did I really want to sell my soul? The future was bleak, but there was no turning back when I received the approval email. To be honest, again, I was hoping to be a finalist instead of a winner. Maybe that was my anxiety talking. Or maybe, I was afraid of success. Failure drives me. Success, well, that scares me. What is there after success?

Within twenty-four hours of approving publication, I noticed on Amazon that there were private retailers offering my book at $55.67. Impossible. I, the author, had yet to even receive a copy of my own book in print form, as I had not ordered a proof copy. Had been confident enough not to delay publication any further and bypassed that step. I filled out an infringement with Amazon against "BOOK IDEAS" and "Good For Readers." Didn't get a response back from the infringement, but I did notice they were taken down except for one from "Good For Readers" at $18.50. By that time my book was available with Amazon at its retail price of $13.99. I hoped anyone who was considering buying my book was smart enough to go with the lower price.

Since I was desperate to try and get the word out, I invested in Tina's Book Promos. I wanted to reach a larger audience in hopes no one was scammed out of purchasing an overpriced book. I can't say for sure investing in Tina's Book Promos really paid off as I didn't really see a spike in sales after the grace period, but at least I did something to get the word out on a platform beyond my own, but don't think I will invest in Tina's Book Promos again.

One thing I wrote about in *How to Stand Up to Bullying* is about my favorite reality show, *Survivor* and how it represents life. I've never felt so strong about participating in any reality television show until *Survivor* came along. Sure, it's beyond my comfort zone and I don't know how to make a fire. When I tell people that I would love to be on the show, their first comments are negative. It's really a reflection of them and that they would never want to be on the show, but they end up putting my dream down. Most people would think maybe they shouldn't try something after they don't get approval from others, however I tend to be the opposite. It fuels my fire that people don't believe in me and I generally like to prove them wrong.

After my grandma passed, I didn't really have anything holding me back anymore. To dream about being on the show and to actually pursue it is completely different. I struggled to make an audition video and questioned that maybe I wasn't cut out for it after all. After several takes on my laptop, I finally made a nice fluid video. When I tried to send it, the file was too big. I almost backed out, but with my mom's aid we figured it out and I sent it in at the end of August 2023. My stomach twisted in so many knots afterwards and I asked out loud, "What did I just do."

I didn't hear back which in a way I was kind of glad. My video wasn't really what they were looking for, I don't believe. It's the experience though that is the most important. You never know if you don't at least try. I finally took a step in the right direction to pursue my dream and that was a big step. I could no longer just say I wanted to be on the show. I actually acted and auditioned. I might not have made the cut the first time, but that's okay because I don't think I was as ready as I believed myself to be. Do I still want to one day be casted on *Survivor?* Absolutely, but only when the time is right. It wasn't my time and I accepted that. Much like in my book *How to Stand Up to Bullying*, actions speak louder than words.

Chapter Nineteen
Chick Lit Café

As a new author, I was paying close attention to everything. As an avid reader, I notice a lot by observation, so I did a lot naturally based on the things I noticed when reading. I joined reader and author groups on Facebook. Commented now and then and tried to promote my own book with some success, but not a lot. One thing I took notice was how popular *Lessons in Chemistry* was trending everywhere I went and had only been released about a year. The book was even mentioned at The Write Stuff writers conference. So, when I came across Chick Lit Café and saw that was one of the books they advertised on their website, I was hooked immediately.

I wanted an opportunity to have a promotional and marketing team to help me make waves with my debut, *The Darkest Side of the Moon*. I thought they could be it. Thought maybe they could give me my big break. The only concern was the price tag, since it wasn't listed on their site. I'm a realist, so I didn't expect an answer after sending in an email. At the time, they seemed legit and a big deal to little old me, an indie author. When I received a response, I was shocked. Not only did they respond, but they approved my book and wanted to work with me. Gave me two different plans to choose from. The first plan was not as extensive as the second plan, which also included a chance to win their book excellence award. Also, their prices were not as outrageous as anticipated. My thought was in the thousands, but it was only in the hundreds.

M. C. Ryder

Although every fiber of my well-being wanted to take the plunge and select the second plan, I played it safe and selected the first plan. At the time, the second plan was overwhelming at what was offered. According to their site, they are based out of Hollywood and even though I wanted the world to know about my books, I wasn't sure if I was truly ready to have a light spotlighted on me yet. I also had a personal matter, my grandma. Her health was failing and the future was unknown. Times were rough and I just wasn't mentally ready for a lot of notice. At least not what plan two detailed.

After my grandma passed, I sent an email informing them that my book was featured in DE MODE Magazine. The managing editor thanked me for the update and asked how DE MODE Magazine found out about my novel. I answered truthfully that I didn't know. I only assumed it was due to one of the reviews posted on Instagram. The marketing manager proceeded to inquire if I invested in a BookLife review, which I did not at the time. I figured since I currently had activity going on with my debut, it was time to invest in a BookLife review, even though it had been against my better judgement, since that was a pricey review. I had not originally planned on investing in one, since I already invested in a review with Chick Lit Café which they had yet to complete.

In May 2023, I won Literary Titan's gold award for *The Darkest Side of the Moon*. I was quick to inform them once more about the award-winning status. My hope, at the time, was for them to move up my book in their waitlist, to complete their own review, and start promoting it while I had buzzworthy stuff going on with my book. It was communicated in the beginning that they had a backlog and I never pushed them to get it done. I was hoping my updates would be incentive enough. Instead, they inquired if I would like to upgrade to plan two. Since my grandma had passed, that opened the door for me. I could now focus on my author career without holding back, so I agreed.

My Journey as an Author

Finally, in June 2023, my book was read and reviewed. I was given a copy of that review in email and loved what they wrote about it. Now that it was finally reviewed, I was eager for them to start promotional services with it. However, I was dismayed when I was informed that I did not have enough Amazon reviews to their liking. At the time, I had nine reviews. I was informed that I should have a minimum of fifteen reviews in order to compel readers to buy my book, and then informed to actually have closer to twenty. Advised that they had a verified Amazon reviewer that they could refer their services and that they "do not make any kind of profit from it." At the end of the email, they put in bold that my book scored "very high" for their book award contest.

I was not fond of the idea of spending more money on reviews for *The Darkest Side of the Moon* as I was mentally done with getting editorial reviews and other reviews from reviewers from Instagram along with family, friends, and coworkers. I felt like I did my part, now it was Chick Lit Café's turn to do their part as I wanted to focus on investing in *A Dance Between Light and Darkness*. I agreed for the managing editor to pass along the verified Amazon reviewer's information, in which the managing editor was cagey with the information.

Instead, I was informed how much the charge was for the review at $169 and each additional review afterwards was $85 for a 5-star Amazon review. I once thought the bookstagram reviewers charging $35 was expensive, which did not include an Amazon review. Now I completely understood why Amazon would be so strict with their guidelines when it comes to reviews, and I agree with it. It doesn't matter how many different ways an individual can claim "you are not paying for a review." If an author has to pay someone to read their book in exchange for a review, then an author is absolutely paying for a review that is posted afterwards!

I reached out to my family, friends, and coworkers in which I gifted my book during Christmas 2022 to post a review on Amazon. When I got my reviews up to 14, after about a week, I reached back out to inform Chick Lit Café. I worked hard to get my reviews up, and they came back stating I didn't have enough "verified reviews" and recommended getting 3 or 4 from the verified Amazon reviewer they knew. I had enough with the stalling. Told them no and asked when I could expect their review to be posted, as well as when their promotional services would begin.

To my disappointment, I was informed that it would take a few weeks or more as they were determining winners for their book excellence award. Had I won Literary Titan before upgrading or known that detail, I wouldn't have upgraded as at the time I wanted a chance to win an award sooner rather than later. Since I already achieved the award-winning status, I didn't care about winning Chick Lit Café's award any longer. I just wanted the promotional services to begin especially when DE MODE Magazine had my book in their magazine as one of the "UNPUTDOWNABLE BOOKS FOR SUMMER 2023."

In that email, it was communicated that the winners would be announced in mid-July "give or take a week." I was not happy with that answer. I was given the option to have them post the information, but I thought I would give them one last chance and perhaps they would make the announcement during the week of my birthday.

Meanwhile, I was doing extensive research into Chick Lit Café. Something I should have done from the beginning. I know, that's on me. Particularly, I reviewed some of the books advertised on their website that won their excellence award. What I found; well, those books did not have the Amazon reviews I had. They had even less. My correspondent at New Book Authors also did some research into them as well and taught me other things to look for that are a red flag and that Chick Lit Café were not what they appeared.

My Journey as an Author

I battled depression when my grandma's health was failing and there was nothing I could do about it except watch her slowly deteriorate. When she passed, I was battling grief. I had good days, but I had a lot of bad days. I went through a traumatic experience and was navigating day-to-day life. It was a relief when she passed, but now I found myself drowning in a sea of despair once more. Slipping back into a depressed state. And you know why? I handed the reins over. I was not in control. When you give control to someone else who does not follow up on their promises, it's so easy to get swept away in the undertow and drown once more.

I performed a Google search at what dates were considered mid-month. The answer I found that was satisfactory to me was the "11th through 20th." So, every day after the 20th of July, I stalked Chick Lit Café's website and socials.

On July 26th, Discourse dropped their book discussion review on *The Darkest Side of the Moon*. Earlier than anticipated. I expected it to drop in early August. The YouTube video generated over a thousand views in one day. As a businesswoman and CEO of my author name, I decided to cut ties with Chick Lit Café on July 27th after they posted a book on their website and it wasn't mine. That was their last chance. I was taking notice of every single book they posted on their website and noticed they seemed to award pretty much all of them at the bottom of the page. I was disgusted and I didn't want to be associated with them anymore. I have the ambition to one day become a successful author and I didn't want them to in any way claim they were responsible for my success. They did not take the news well when asking for a refund. I was firm in telling them that I was dissatisfied with the amount of time it was taking before promotional marketing began, four months, and how assertive they were in pushing other author review services onto me to generate additional 5-star Amazon reviews.

The response I received, once it was clear my mind was made up, "you are pulling an age-old scam on us." My mouth literally dropped. I could not believe they had the audacity to say that in an email. Very unprofessional and reinforced that I made the right decision. In my response back, I kept it professional and informed them that I don't tolerate name calling, and referenced my latest published book, *How to Stand Up to Bullying*. I talked the talk. Now I had to walk the walk.

I was grateful that I went to a few writing conferences where I met an actual lawyer who's also a fiction author. I used that to my advantage, knowing who I could turn to as a last resort. Gave them a choice. The easy way or the hard way. Little did I know that I also had a team member from New Book Authors who had a background in legal, and sought out advice as I wrote email responses when Chick Lit Café fired off unprofessional ones. They let their emotions take over while I kept my cool.

Chick Lit Café chose the hard way. I gave them the option of keeping my mouth shut about my dissatisfaction with their services. That wasn't enough for them to come to a compromise with a refund I deserved. Although I asked for a full refund, I would have settled for a percentage if it was fair. What they offered me was less than half which was unacceptable to me as I had nothing to show for using their services which I stated. They even confirmed what I already knew, "you did not generate any sales because we didn't get to the part where we actually market your book."

My debut, *The Darkest Side of the Moon*, was added to their website back in March once I paid, in which I would have been willing to pay their fee for advertising on their website even though no sales were generated from it being featured on their site. I also would have been willing to pay a fraction of what they charge for their book review, however, they were greedy and wanted the full price of $299.00. The problem with the review they wrote up was, they never posted it on their website, so it did not exist other than in email correspondence and could not be verified. I was waiting patiently for the day I could update my socials and

My Journey as an Author

Amazon Author page in the editorial review section with their review. That day, unfortunately, never came.

Upon further review of Chick Lit Café's home page it states, "Chick Lit Café participates in the affiliation program at Amazon. We may receive commissions for books purchased on this site." Make what you want of that.

Once it became clear, I was not going to be able to come to a peaceful resolution with Chick Lit Café, I immediately called my credit card company. When I got the credit card company involved, I ceased all contact with Chick Lit Café. When they became aware the 3rd party was involved, they reached out offering $210.00 as a refund. I paid $420.00 in March 2023 for plan 1 and then updated to plan 2 in May 2023 with a payment of $386.99. You do the math.

A week later, when it was clear to them that I wasn't agreeing to their offer, they sent a nasty email stating I "threatened to sue," then "don't bother responding," and that I had "taken this to a whole other level." This, my friends, is classic bullying. Someone doesn't get what they want and they go off the rails, turning it around making you the bad guy. Although at the time of reading the email I was beyond angry, I also knew it was a ply to get me to respond back. If you read *How to Stand Up to Bullying* this is where "silence is an answer" comes into play. Two days later, I visited my Goodreads page only to find a 1-star review that happened to be the same day as the email. Coincidence? That's up to you to decide. A few days later, it was taken down. No worries, I have a screenshot for my records.

To other authors, especially independent authors, reading this, do your homework before not after. Some businesses are out to profit from unknowing authors, who are eager to be the next big-name author. I only hope Chick Lit Café learned a valuable lesson. Oh, and apparently, I won first place, according to the director himself, however when they submitted documentation when I opened a dispute with my credit card company, they claimed in the notes section that I "got mad when she didn't win." So, which one was it? I'll never know.

Chapter Twenty
Red Flags

In the publishing world, there are several different breeds of scammers. There are so many that at some point in a writer's life, they will fall victim to them. Everyone has a voice they want heard. Everyone has a story they want to share and enthrall readers. Going from writer to author is just the first step. Every author goes into the business wanting to succeed. Wanting readers to invest in their story. Dream of becoming a bestseller and making big bucks. One learns really fast that it's a full-time job that doesn't guarantee solid income.

The first scam is the publishing process itself.

There are so many "publishing" companies out there that are eager for motivated writers who want to get their work out into the world. When a writer gets a response back that a "publisher" is interested in publishing their work, it's like winning the lottery. All a writer can think about is they won. Little do they know that them paying the publisher hundreds or thousands of dollars is not the way it works. If it's poetry, the poem gets included in an anthology with other poems in which the writer pays to have a copy of the book of poetry their poem is featured in. As a young writer, I participated in exactly that. Guess what, the only ones who bought the book are the authors themselves. Does that collection of poetry get marketed to readers out in the world? No.

Editors are the next that are not always what they seem. They provide services and don't deliver on deadlines. I have not walked this road, but I have done some research in which the prices are extreme. It's hard to get a sense of an individual online. One site I did research was Reedsy. I ended up finding a potential, who is also an author and we're still connected, however didn't follow through as I was given positive feedback on my writing and editing capabilities that I needed at the time. It gave me the confidence to not invest in the extra expense. Are my stories without flaws? No, but even authors who are published by the name houses still have editing errors. I may not be perfect, but it's the story that matters, how readers connect to it, not the minor edits missed.

Social media. In this day and age, the one certain free way to spread awareness is through social media. There are many alternatives. As an author, it's important to have Goodreads. The other ways are Facebook, Twitter, Instagram, Pinterest, TikTok, and YouTube. There are many other places too, Threads is something new, but those are the main. One can make an account for all or some. It's up to the author's discretion and who their target audience is. However, with social media, you are opening a can of worms for more scammers to target you. While one is trying to get the word out about their book(s), individuals are targeting for their own benefits. When someone reaches out to you, that you don't know, keep your guard up. If they are flattering you that they have a "passion" for writers, or writing is an "admirable" quality to have, they are buttering you up to tear down your walls. Asking for your book link is a red flag. If they are truly interested in your craft and admire your art, they should be able to find that information on your page if you have everything there that anyone needs to know about how to get one of your books. There is a term called pirating. Be mindful who you trust with valuable information, as there are always scammers ready to profit off of you without your awareness.

The biggest downside to social media is reviews. Ever hear of bookstagram? It's a known tread on Instagram where people review and post about books. Some are legit. Some you should question. I've had multiple individuals reach out to me about reviewing my book. In the beginning, despite my better judgement, I took the risk and agreed. I was paying them to read my book and post about it. It's really the opposite of what an author should be doing. Not paying the reader to read my book. There is a reason Amazon has strict rules. I ensured the ones I worked with did not post on Amazon. It worked in my favor. I'm convinced it's how DE MODE Magazine discovered me and reached out. The problem was, once I gave in to one, I had more knocking on my door. Some were even "bestselling" authors. Also, each time I posted about my book, I had others commenting and telling me where to promote my book on a page that had a million followers. I resisted in the beginning, but when I wanted to get the word out about an Amazon scam, I caved and promoted with one. The individual warned me that I would get a lot of direct messages from those not in it for the right reasons. After the post, I had a boost of "followers." When I ignored them and as days went by, the number of "followers" dropped.

Reviews. Every business in this world relies heavily on authentic reviews to help spread the word about their business. Reviews can either make you or break you. They also bring one positivity that they made a difference in someone's life. As for the negative ones, most of the time it's people who have a chip on their shoulders. I never take 1-star reviews seriously. I gravitate to the 2-star or 3-star reviews. In the publishing industry, reviews help sell books to readers. How many books do you pick up that have reviews by other authors, even named authors? Perhaps a named author that has a review flashed on the cover will capture a reader's interest, but I know for a fact that is not the decision for me to read a book.

There are many places an author can go to get a review. What the business has to offer with the review is what you should pay attention to. The top in the business is Kirkus, Publisher's Weekly, Booklife, and Readers' Favorite. Kirkus costs the most. The question you should ask, though, what do you get with an expensive review? Does it reach your target audience? A well-written review is great to flash for your book's creditability, but let's face it, you PAID for that review.

In the case with Chick Lit Café, part of my payment included a review by them. That, yes, they did deliver in my inbox, however it was never published, so theoretically it did not exist, therefore I could never use it. I never heard of Chick Lit Café until I was in the business of trying to market my book and stumbled across their name and viewed their website. The homework that I didn't do at the time was pay attention to minor details. I saw what I wanted to see. They had current trending books on their website. They had a lot of repetitive "sharing is caring." I looked for their business with the BBB however, they were not listed with any negatives. I looked through their author testimonials, but that was of course all positive. I looked for any negative reviews on their social media or by a Google search, but came up empty. That lead me to take a chance with them, but that also was a red flag I neglected to see. No business is without flaws. No business meets everyone's expectations. Furthermore, I learned how to view on Facebook in the about section to see what ads were running in the page transparency. When taking a look, no ads were ever run by Chick Lit Café. When I did try to file a BBB report against them, I found there was no address listed anywhere. What business does not have an address, even if it's a P.O. Box?

Unfortunately, red flags can be staring you in the face, but you have to learn the hard way to grow in how to avoid them. There will always be those who want to deceive you in order to profit. Don't ever be quick to rush into anything because there is a time limit. That is a solid red flag. Writing a book is a success. Everyone else is just looking for a way to profit off of your success.

Chapter Twenty-One
Literary Titan and Discourse

I was scrolling through a Facebook group when I saw an image of a cover with a Literary Titan award sticker. Never heard of Literary Titan so searched for their website. Liked what I saw right away. Not only could I gain another editorial Amazon review, but also had the possibility of winning an award sooner rather than later before the summer 2023 season started. Most importantly, they were within my reasonable budget for an editorial review. Not only that, but they also posted their reviews on their website, socials, and additional sites including Barnes & Noble, Goodreads, and BookBub.

There was more value in that singular editorial review than the well-known in the literary world, like Kirkus Reviews, Readers' Favorite, and Booklife.

I entered my first three books, *The Darkest Side of the Moon, A Dance Between Light and Darkness,* and *A Darker Demise,* all at the same time. When I received each review, I was beyond happy with how each review turned out. I also had the opportunity to answer some interview questions for each of my books. Another win. Finally, I could answer questions about my writing process and talk about my books! Something I've been craving. Not only did I get excellent reviews, but on June 2, 2023 I found out that not only did I win one award with Literary Titan, I won an award for all three of my books!

I looked into creating a book trailer and asked some questions. Writing in the YA genre, I knew I needed to get something out on YouTube since a good chunk of my audience hangs out there, me included. I just didn't have the resources to create visually appealing content and was still brainstorming, doing something different from what's already out there.

Literary Titan offers many services other than just an editorial review for all kinds of authors and their needs. What an author may be looking for, Literary Titan most certainly can provide, including a video book review on YouTube. It just so happened Literary Titan partnered with Discourse at the right time when I was looking into my YouTube approach.

While I was patiently waiting for Chick Lit Café to start their marketing of my debut, *The Darkest Side of the Moon*, I decided to make the investment for the Discourse book discussion as I had noticed that was becoming a trend. By this time, I was really investing more money than I had planned. Not only had I invested with Chick Lit Café's marketing services, but I also invested in Booklife's editorial review, which was over my reasonable budget for a review. Editorial reviews are great, if readers take the time to read them, but they are more for the publishing industry. Many readers don't take the time to really read reviews unless they are interested in reading the book. Without constant news about a book, readers are not going to pay attention.

While I was waiting for the Discourse YouTube video to drop, I was waiting for Chick Lit Café to start their marketing. It was a time where it was completely out of my control. I had to twiddle my thumbs and wait. I know how to be patient. The expected time for the Discourse video was within 45 days, which I calculated to be early August. I was hoping to time things right that by the time Chick Lit Café started their marketing, the Discourse video would drop soon after and build more momentum for beach readers.

The summer season had just begun for 2023 and not only did I win an award with Literary Titan, but I was also featured in DE MODE Magazine. I had a lot of accomplishments under my belt in under a year in which my debut was released. Had it not been for DE MODE Magazine reaching out to me when they did at the time, I mentally was going to take a break from it all. It was like a universal sign urging me to not stop despite my personal circumstances. So, I did the opposite of what I was going to do. I pushed myself and invested against my better judgement. Something had to pan out, eventually.

Near the end of July, Discourse dropped their book discussion on YouTube earlier than I had anticipated. It took them around 30 days instead of 45 days. An unexpected surprise. The moment my phone indicated that a new YouTube video I'd be interested in, since of course I now followed Discourse, and saw my book plastered on the icon of the video, I froze. I just stared at the video notification as my heart skipped several beats. Reading a review someone wrote, even if it's a good review, is in a way biased. I paid for that review and it may be honest, but it's hard to tell how authentic that individual's review is since you are unable to view facial expressions. Now I had two people, who I did not know other than what I saw in their videos, discussing my book. Yes, I paid for their services and they might be gentle, but what I now had was the nonverbal cue aspect. I was terrified! I wanted to watch immediately, but also held back. When I finally mustered the courage, I watched.

I watched intently while holding my breath. Observed and listened to more than how they discussed my book. I paid attention to a lot of detail. More than I'm sure anyone does with any of their video discussions. I wanted to know for sure if they really did enjoy reading my book or if they were forcing themselves to say nice things about it. There were little tidbits I picked up on that eased my mind gradually. I laughed out loud when they mentioned asparagus. They hit on good points, didn't give any major spoilers, and I was sad when it came to an end. I immediately watched it again and again and again. Forwarded the link to my family and friends. Over the moon how it turned out, yes pun intended! My night ended with a huge positive.

The next day, I emailed Chick Lit Café to terminate services with them. They let me down, again. I gave them one too many chances to get their act together. This time I did not inform them of my book's update. No way was I going to let them profit any more than they already had and claim they helped me become a successful author. To anyone reading this who is part of the Chick Lit Café circle, that is the bitter truth of why I abandoned ship. Had nothing to do with winning or not winning the excellence award. Had nothing to do with "scamming" for an editorial review. It was strictly a business decision.

While I do not support Chick Lit Café's business, I do 100% support Literary Titan and Discourse. When one collaborates with another business and their services and continues to return, that speaks volumes. And I did collaborate with Discourse again for *A Dance Between Light and Darkness*.

I was brimming with happiness and excitement and emailed Literary Titan the next day about how much I enjoyed Discourse's book discussion on *The Darkest Side of the Moon*. My observations were confirmed that Discourse did in fact enjoy my book and was hoping for book two. I took a gamble. Hoped I would be refunded by Chick Lit Café so I could turn around and put that money to good use, but there was no guarantee I would get the full amount. I'm mindful of spending money I don't have and paying it off later. I had to believe everything would work out in my favor, so before knowing for sure I invested in a Discourse video for book two. When *All I See Are Dark Clouds* and *The Neighbors* were published, I took another risky gamble and purchased a Discourse video for each book. Little did I know that I would end up losing my dispute case with Chick Lit Café and not get a cent refunded.

When *A Dance Between Light and Darkness* dropped, I didn't hesitate to listen to the book discussion. Absolutely loved the intro. Laughed out loud again with some of the theatrics. Delighted Niles received a spotlight as I had a blast writing his character. I was a little disappointed that the views weren't there like they were for my first book. For a 10-minute video, Discourse guarantees over 4k views, which was achieved, but *The Darkest Side of the Moon* broke that record within 2 weeks right out of the gate. Now I was second guessing if I made the right decision in investing in book discussion videos with my other two books. Were their viewers already sick of me?

The next video Discourse dropped was a different book, *A Pain in the Gut,* by a different author who also used Literary Titan's services as I noted the award sticker. When it was dropped the views gained over 4k in a matter of a couple of days. Once it slowed, they dropped another book that didn't gain as many views before another, which I was surprised didn't gain as many views either, since it had a captivating cover. I was second-guessing myself. I purchased the more expensive book review that guarantees 6k views. Even if I didn't make 6k, I was hoping for a bit more reviews than what *The Darkest Side of the Moon* gained at the time, which slowed at 4.7k.

I was leaving Oregon Dairy's Corn Maze when I received the notification. When I got in the car, I let the video play. Glad they gave a spoiler warning in the beginning because if one does not read the books in order there are spoilers, but at the same time if they are read out of order and a reader enjoyed the book, they may just want to read them all. I was thrilled Leo got a spotlight. Until Discourse, only one reviewer mentioned Leo in which I thought he would be a fan favorite, when I actually had some fans.

Within 24 hours, the views skyrocketed. At first it was a slow go, but once views caught on there was a new book discussion video by Discourse, there were over 4k in no time. Also, what I found humbling was the amount of likes the video received. Over 400. I stalked all the other videos and the most likes were around 120. Turns out their viewers were not sick of my books. Now I had *The Neighbors* to anticipate.

A few days later, *The Neighbors* dropped. At first it was slow in gaining views, but by the second day it exploded with views. The day after, Firebird Book Awards announced the winners in each category in which *The Neighbors* placed 2nd place in New Adult Fiction. I posted about my book on social and included the Discourse video in the link which Pat Rullo retweeted. By the weekend the video gained 9.1K views! The most of all my books. The video, as always, was nicely done and had me laughing. I was sad my fun was coming to an end until 2024.

Chapter Twenty-Two
All I See Are Dark Clouds

When the idea for my first story, *The Darkest Side of the Moon* came to me, I hadn't planned on writing more. Had years to develop the story in my mind. Referenced parts of myself and my one childhood friend into the relationship between Nadine and Camille. However, both were their own character, which was clear as their characters developed. As time moved on, more seeds were planted into Camille's characterization.

The story developed beyond just one story. I did not have a clear direction at first. Only one scene that replayed. A scene that I had for a long time that was its own story. I just didn't know it was tied in to what became The Dark series. Before I could tell Camille's story, I had to write the middle story. After I wrote *A Dance Between Light and Darkness,* the direction of the third story made a lot more sense. The first two started out with no rhyme or reason, but the third I had a clear direction that steered me on what it was about.

Depression.

Writing a character in such a low state was daunting. At the time I wrote the story, I did not know what it was to be truly depressed. We all have our days without sun. I had to sink deeper into that mindset in order for it be realistic. I'm grateful I had many days of abundant sunshine to help me stay afloat. It's kind of depressing writing a depressed character. If you're not careful, you can sink. Writing the story came with a lot of breaks. I had to in order to keep my sanity.

M. C. Ryder

Every artist in the world, no matter what kind of art they choose to craft, always has a masterpiece. I've been writing pretty much my entire life. I've written many short stories, poems, and even lyrics. The stories developed over time. I didn't write a full-length novel until late in my teenage years. I love all my stories. They each have a special place in my heart. I can remember all the feels in crafting them, like a song that takes you back to your memorable moments in your life.

This story, *All I See Are Dark Clouds*, I consider a masterpiece. It's the longest story I have ever written, to date. With each story I wrote, I always strived to make them longer. Set small goals. When I started this project, length wasn't on my mind. I just wanted it long enough to be considered a novel. This story could have been even longer, but I cut myself off. Feared it would end up being too long. Even though it could have continued on and on and on, I saw an opportunity where I could do a time jump and leave you, the reader, on the edge of your seat. Even I was on the edge of my seat.

Again, a minor character surprised me. Michael. He ended up not being so minor after all. In fact, halfway through, I jumped back into *A Dance Between Light and Darkness* and added more details for his character. I had that luxury since I had yet to proceed in starting the publication process. The main reason my prior stories never made it to publication is because they sit incomplete. Although I do have finished stories, there's still an aspect in them that is not. I do not rush. I take my time. If I'm going to write a trilogy, I have to complete all three before even considering publishing. If I can't finish all three, then I won't publish. Simple as that. I've read a lot of series where it was clear that the author was rushed and the story lost its spark. Moral of the story, if you are a writer, take your time.

Another character that surprised me was Jerry. He was only going to be referenced once and then put in the corner, but Jerry didn't want to stay in the corner. I found I kept circling back to his character and when it came time to write an intense scene, he was my savior. I never saw it coming until I found myself backed into a corner. When the lightbulb lit above my head, I was in awe. There was a reason why he kept making noise. Listen to your characters. Good stories tend to write themselves as long as you are receptive.

In order for stories to be believable, research is a necessity. I am more confident incorporating elements that I have no clue about because I have access to the world wide web. I am not Spanish. I have never been to Spain. I am not an expert in the culture. What I do know is how to navigate Google. It still amazes me that people can ask a question, out loud, but not search for an answer when answers are so quick these days at a few keystrokes. Of course, you can't always believe the first answer that pops up. You have to dig a little. I only hope I honored the Spanish community in the right way in incorporating Iris's character.

As it so happens, an element from a future story allowed me to share a bond with one of my mom's coworkers. Went out to dinner and met with her. In casual conversation, she was willing to ask her boyfriend, who is fluent in Spanish, about the correct wording. I'm thankful this journey allows strangers to come together and help each other out. All I want is to be as accurate as possible, but I can be reserved in asking because I don't want to appear ignorant or be taken advantage of.

I'm not shy about including diversity. It's challenging and harder to write. I do like challenges. I make the best decisions I can for my stories. Even something so simple as what's for breakfast. Tostada. Let me tell you something. It's delicious! I went through a phase where I couldn't get enough of it. Until I had one too many. Writing is a lot of things. It's therapeutic, rewarding, and a learning experience.

Beckett was an unusual character to write. At the time, I thought the concept was sublime, but by the time I reached it, I had second thoughts. Was I taking things too far? What were people going to think? I had to reflect. Go with the flow as I slowly pieced the scenes together, cringing. I was so eager to get to the scenes and then I hit a wall. I thought it would be the end. That I would give up. Stop writing and never finish like so many before, but I didn't. I kept going. I came too far to stop. Maybe I would just be a laughingstock. There are no rewards without risks. In the end, what I managed to accomplish was beautiful in its own sense. I'm glad I stuck by it. Even if it's not received well, it was necessary for the story. Time will tell.

I always knew how the scene between Camille and Beckett was going to play out, but when I finally wrote it, I doubled over in hysterical laughter. I never laughed so hard for so long before. When I finally got my composure, glowing alien eyes were staring at me. My cats. I doubled over again in laughter. At the time, I didn't have in mind what Camille's reaction was going to be, but since I couldn't stop laughing, I wrote it in. And I'm laughing as I type this. I mean, if it's real and authentic for the author to have that kind of reaction, surely the readers would too, right?

Forgiveness was a theme in *A Dance Between Light and Darkness* and carried over. It was also my elephant in the room. I avoided it for a long time until I had to face it. It actually came sooner than I expected and I thought I reached it too soon. I had to dive deep and think how the story was more than just overcoming grief, depression, and finding forgiveness. It was also a story about moving on. Breaking free of that weight Camille carried and finding herself again. When it came time to address the imperative moment, it was authentic. The answer was always there, staring me in the face. I just didn't see it. Funny how one word can be so powerful.

Defiant.

Exactly what this series represents. Taking things to the next level. Daring to be different. Crafting dynamic stories that leave a lasting impression that is also meaningful. That hopefully makes you, the reader, stop and truly embrace the words you read. If I only affect one life with my stories, then I did my job. I already know I changed mine.

Chapter Twenty-Three
The Neighbors

There was a period of time in my life when I worked with some nurses who did office work. They are the kindest souls and get overlooked because they are at the bottom of the totem pole. They are smart and caring individuals and helpful. Although I never worked with a maternity nurse, Zoe being a maternity nurse was necessary for my story.

Again, I thought I bit off more than I could chew. I do not have first-hand experience with what it's like to give childbirth. Never been in that environment. I'm not one who likes to ask a lot of questions. I feel like I'm a bother. Thankfully, I have the internet and people who like to be vocal on it. I put in a lot of thought and hard work to create a believable atmosphere. My mom was the expert. She had me. When she was reading it, she asked me how I came up with some of the material. I executed what I was going for well, since I took her back to that time when she had me. If it's believable to her, then I had to do something right.

In all of my stories, there is always a character that surprises me. That character was Anne. She is a blend of teachers from my childhood, but I took her a step further. I only needed her to open up a bank account for Zoe. That was where I was going to leave Anne, but like many of my other characters, she didn't stay quiet in the background. She kept popping up. I went with the flow. She ended up being a very important character. More than a teacher. One who helped shape Zoe. Teachers can rejoice!

My Journey as an Author

When I finished *All I See Are Dark Clouds,* I was excited for another opportunity to write in second-person narrative. This time it wasn't a story about Nadine. Although Zoe is Nadine 2.0, in my mind, I took Zoe to the next level. Love how Zoe turned out. Love her sass. Love the dynamic between her and Terrence. It was so much fun to write. There was a scene I envisioned that didn't make it. When I was younger, I used to play basketball. One day, taking a mental break to shoot some hoops, a scene popped into my mind between Zoe and Terrence playing some basketball along with Jensen. Unfortunately, the opportunity never presented itself and the scene was never written as it just didn't fit.

I always knew *The Neighbors* was a short story to tie-in with *All I See Are Dark Clouds*, but I could have kept writing more. Debated if I should just make it into a full-length novel. That wasn't my goal. It was the longest short story I wrote for the series, at that time. There was much more I could have dived into, but once I found the opportunity to tie it up, I did. Sometimes the short stories are the best. So far, all of my short stories came out brilliantly. I'm still in awe that I wrote them.

Running. Not my thing. I'm more of a sprinter. Writing about Zoe running all the time did inspire me to get out there and do a little more running myself. For a hot minute, I thought maybe I would sign up for a mini marathon. That was short-lived. Ha-ha. I don't like to set myself up for disappointment. And yes, I did my running at night. Like I said, more of a sprint. You won't see me running straight through for miles.

I didn't plan on Zoe being a control freak. I was just trying to fill up some pages of what she did when she was not at work. Again, I just went with the flow. I let her take the lead. It was her story, after all. I will admit, out of all of my strong female characters, I think Zoe is the best. She has spunk and doesn't let any guy get away with anything.

Even though she is a strong woman, sometimes, like all strong women out there, she still needs help. Strong women aren't born strong. They don't get strong overnight. They view hard situations differently and use determination to get out of those situations. Like the great Albert Einstein once said, "Where there's a will, there's a way." Always.

The scene when Zoe was attacked was gut twisting. When I write my stories, I am in the same atmosphere as my characters. I feel what they feel. Fear what they fear. To me writing is like acting. You have to go into a different mind space. So, I was in the bedroom with Zoe. I was mentally fighting back, like Zoe. Trying to escape knowing what was going to happen if we didn't. After the scene, I had to take a break and go for a walk and de-escalate.

Not only is writing like acting, but writing is a teaching opportunity, and also a learning one. A lot of thought goes into my stories. I don't like to write the same thing twice. I've written other scenes that were similar, so I had to do something a little different to keep it fresh. I was satisfied how I executed it.

I'm not sure if anyone picked up on it. I know my mom didn't, but when Zoe stopped being strict to her routines, that ended up saving her life. Like a lot of other minor things, that had not been planned, it came naturally. In my mind, if she would have kept to her routines, I envision she would have ended up being one of Camille's victims.

Like all my other stories, I had to piece this one together until I saw the big picture. Again, it came back to love and hate. Zoe grew up in a place she hated and felt worthless. Due to that environment, she developed scars. The big question I had to ask myself was why did Zoe choose to become a maternity nurse to begin with? I didn't know the answer right away. I just kept writing until I got to the part when I finally had to answer that question. When I did, not only was it brilliant, but so very sad at the same time. Makes me wonder about actual maternity nurses or just nurses in general. Sometimes we don't truly know the root of our decisions in our career paths. What drives us? What are we looking for? What don't we have in our lives that we try to get elsewhere?

The greatest mystery of all.

Chapter Twenty-Four
Booklife

Before Chick Lit Café, I checked out Booklife. I wasn't fond of the pricy review at $399, so I put that on hold. I did create an account, and I did purchase to promote my book on their site as well as Publishers Weekly site as a marketing tool. Nothing against Booklife or Publishers Weekly, but for me it wasn't a good investment. I didn't generate any sales, and within a day or two my book fell off the first page, as every known author on this earth also promotes their book for their fifteen seconds of fame. Most authors know that Publishers Weekly and Booklife is the place to go.

It wasn't until Chick Lit Café inquired if I had invested in a Booklife review was when I took action. Since I was building quite a resume with *The Darkest Side of the Moon*, I felt this was the right time to invest despite already investing more than I intended in a span of a few months. I was actually surprised how well the review turned out. Got more A's than B's. Of all the places to score a B, the cover was not what I predicted.

Booklife gave me a confidence boost. After it was included in the magazine, I even had a publicist reach out to me. After careful consideration and advice from trusted sources, I decided not to pursue the publicist. With my name starting to get out in the publishing world, I had to be cautious how I proceeded to avoid scams.

On a high, I made the decision to pursue the Booklife Prize contest. An opportunity for more buzz for my book and a chance to win a grand prize of $5,000. When I received my assessment, that's when I heard genuine negativity about my book, *The Darkest Side of the Moon*. I didn't expect to get 10/10, but it was hard to receive an overall score of 6.25 out of 10.

As months passed, I waited patiently for the opportunity to send an email for the indie spotlight at a chance to be included as August's Summer Reads Part 3: Sci-fi/Fantasy. As soon as I could, the first day in July I sent the email. Later on, when I decided to cut ties with Chick Lit Café, I had emailed again to remove any mention of Chick Lit Café. I wanted no connections with Chick Lit Café whatsoever and included in the email that I understood if my multiple emails disqualified me. When August arrived and they finally posted the list, I wasn't surprised I hadn't made the cut.

Not only had I invested in a review for my first book, but also my second, *A Dance Between Light and Darkness*. Again, the review came out positive with a B for the cover. I won't lie, that hurt a bit. I spent so much time trying to find the right cover image to capture the theme of the story and everyone who saw the cover were blown away. I'm proud of that cover whatever the "experts" say.

When I received my assessment report for the Booklife Prize contest for *A Dance Between Light and Darkness*, some I expected to score low in, but compared to my first book I was hoping to achieve higher than a 6.50 out of 10.

Despite the disappointment, and against my better judgement, I decided to put *All I See Are Dark Clouds* and *The Neighbors* into the Booklife Prize ring. I won't lie, my first two books I was finding my way, but the stories and my writing really took off by book three and beyond. I was hoping I would achieve higher scores. Maybe not a perfect 10, but close to it.

When the email came for *All I See Are Dark Clouds*, I was disappointed once again. I achieved a higher score from my first two, but only 7 out of 10. It became clear to me then that I didn't have what the experts were looking for. Although I was disappointed, that wasn't going to stop me from trying to get my books into as many hands as I could. At the end of the day, the "experts" don't have the final say, the readers do. It didn't seem likely I had a chance to win the final prize. To be honest, I kind of didn't want to win that amount of money anyway. Initially, I had no plans to compete for the prize. Of course, it would have been an honor if I had, but it also would have had the wrong individuals knocking on my door.

The last hope I had to achieve a score of 8 or higher rested with *The Neighbors*. When I finally received the email, I was discouraged to receive a lower score than *All I See Are Dark Clouds* at 6.25 out of 10.

Since this is my journey as an author, and my experiences, I've determined Booklife is a bad investment for me. The "experts" don't appreciate my works. It's clear to me I don't have what they are looking for. Will that prevent me from pursuing reviews and submitting into the Booklife Prize. Yes. Will I completely eliminate them? No. When I have a story worth sharing with Booklife, I'll see what the experts say, but they won't stop me from my passion, writing.

Chapter Twenty-Five
Firebird Book Awards

I don't recall what Facebook group or book I saw the Firebird Book Award seal on which led me to make the search. I'm going to be honest here, I would go to bookstores and eye every award seal for ideas about what competitions to enter. Many I would dismiss if there was a potential I would have to travel if I won since I'm not in the position to travel. Don't get me wrong, I want to travel, I just don't have the resources yet. Many I was not qualified for since I was an independent author.

I was blown away when I took a look at the Speak Up Talk Radio website. Not only was there an opportunity to win an award, but unlike others I entered, the contest had a charity twist and an opportunity to speak on the Authors on Fire Podcast. This was after my incident with Chick Lit Café and I was trying to cut back on spending, but I couldn't pass on the opportunity and knowing even if I didn't win, my money was going to a good cause. There are more who are less fortunate than me and could only hope my stories had the power to connect with someone low in life and perhaps lift them up.

So, I entered. I already had the award-winning status, so I wasn't after that. My eye was on the opportunity to speak to a large audience, and hopefully get the word out beyond algorithms on the internet. It was a shorter waiting period than the other competitions I entered that I wouldn't hear the results until the end of November. I entered each of my books in The Dark series once, and entered *How to Stand Up to Bullying* three times in hopes of the top award. I didn't do much promotion as I figured that would speak for itself. I did enter *How to Stand Up to Bullying* into the All-Author cover of the month contest for September, and knew I was going to really promote it in October for National Bullying Prevention Month, so it would have been perfect if it happened to win when the Firebird Book Awards were announced in October.

Unfortunately, *How to Stand Up to Bullying* did not win the top prize, which at the time I was disappointed. As I scrolled through the list, at first, I didn't think I won in any category since I only entered each of my books in The Dark series once. I believed my odds were not as good since there were way more books entered and possibly in multiple categories. I scrolled faster just to get to the end and nearly missed when the first win revealed itself. I had to scroll back up to the Fantasy category and looked closer, realizing my book *A Dance Between Light and Darkness* had placed 3rd. I was in disbelief. Out of all my books I didn't think that would be the one to place as it seemed to get overlooked a lot.

I continued to scroll for a period of time again before my eyes landed on *The Neighbors* which placed 2nd in the New Adult Fiction category. I was delighted as Discourse had just dropped their book discussion.

I scrolled a tiny bit more before landing on *The Darkest Side of the Moon,* which placed 1st in New Fiction (first time published). By this time, I started to see a pattern. Could it be that I placed for *all* of my books in The Dark series? Yes! *A Darker Demise* placed 3rd in Short Stories and *All I See Are Dark Clouds* placed 3rd in Young Adult Fiction.

When I got to the Honorable Recognition, I saw that *How to Stand Up to Bullying* was on the list. As I processed the reason why it didn't place in the three categories that I had selected, I thought about the content. It's only about 70 pages. It's very short and there are books that exceed that which are deserving.

After I got over the disappointment in *How to Stand Up to Bullying* not doing as well as I had hoped, it finally hit me that all five of my books in *The Dark* series had placed. I was now a two-time award-winning author! I scrolled back through to make sure it wasn't a trick of my eyes. It wasn't. All five had placed. That I had not predicted!

I really wanted an opportunity to have a voice beyond the pages, so I searched back through the site and found there were options to purchase and schedule a time slot. Again, the money was going to a good cause and it would have been foolish of me *not* to schedule an author interview with the Authors on Fire Podcast. It was an opportunity I had been waiting for, to finally get a chance to talk about my books.

Everything I wanted to know was included on their Q & A on their author series link. It didn't chase away the nerves though. I liked that I could request the questions before the interview took place, so I could mentally prepare. Pat Rullo has this calming energy she projects in her emails and in her voice as I listened to several different ones to prepare.

When the big day came, I was over-prepared mentally and just wanted to get it done and over with, but at the same time, the nerves took control. I knew what all I wanted to say and wrote down a few key points I wanted to express, but I didn't want to read from a script. Didn't want to sound robotic.

If there is one thing to calm me down, it's speaking about my passion of cats which I shared with Pat Rullo. That had not been part of the questions forwarded to me, but that was something I could talk about without over-analyzing if I'm speaking the right words to convey my message.

I won't lie, I got tongue tied at parts. I'm thankful technology is capable of cutting certain parts, but I did say "umm" and "you know" a lot. It annoyed me. It was my first time. Even though Pat Rullo had a way to make me feel relaxed in conversation with her, when I never met her, there was also a part of my mind pinging that hundreds, thousands, or even millions of people would have the opportunity to listen to my interview. I wanted to reach as many as I could, but at the same time, it's daunting. I'm an introvert. I don't like the spotlight.

However, if I want people to read my books, they have to know they exist as there are a sea of books out there all competing with each other to be read. I have to do something to stand out. To encourage readers to invest their time to reading my craft. If you want to eventually be successful, you have to step outside of your comfort zone. I took that step and even though I don't like hearing my voice replayed, it was also a learning oppertunity. I can't grow if I don't know what to work on. Now that the first vocal interview was completed, the sky was the limit and I looked forward to improving myself.

Chapter Twenty-Six
Weight Loss

All my life I've experienced the yo-yo effect in losing and gaining weight. Of being mindful that I was "overweight." On the inside, I never felt like I was overweight, but my clothing size told me otherwise. I was pretty active in my younger years. Walked home from school every day, which was between half a mile to a mile away, as I switched from elementary to middle to high school. Played basketball during my younger days. I could run sprints. Could run on the basketball court back and forth, but when it came to running a mile straight on, I couldn't run it completely.

At least, not in under five minutes. All I could think about was that the end was so far away and I would give up to walk in between. On the basketball court, my goal was to keep the ball in sight. Having a purpose versus being forced to do something has completely different mindsets.

When I was bored, I mindlessly ate. My hunger was never satisfied; I'd eat more. Felt guilty when I indulged on the things that weren't healthy options. Overwhelmed with the fact that beverages hid a ton of calories. So much I should not have. So much I should have instead. I resented the healthy options. They didn't satisfy me. I didn't like them.

I joined a weight loss group. Learned about portion control and how to count calories and be mindful of what to eat. In the beginning, I was successful, but then I reached a point where the weight stopped coming off and I mentally checked out, which caused the weight to go right back on.

Like many others, I joined a gym. Busted my butt with little to no results. Gave it my all for at least an hour. Hated walking a fast pace on a treadmill, sometimes running, going nowhere. Hated the elliptical just as much. Lifted weights. I despised the repetitive routine that felt like I accomplished nothing.

My first job was physical. Required a lot of walking, especially as I climbed the ladder and gained more responsibilities. Got short breaks and often times ate quick slices of pizza to get through. Not a very nutritious meal. I thought I would shed the weight. When I was working, I wasn't eating mindlessly. Yet, I didn't lose much. Didn't gain much either. Stayed neutral. Was I completely fit? No, but I wasn't overly out of shape either. So many times, during the course of my life, I felt like a skinny girl trapped in an oversized bodysuit. I could do more things than others my size or who were more overweight. It just didn't make sense to me how, at times, I could stay in control and still gain weight. Sometimes it was like I just looked at food and gained. I saw a different person in the mirror from the few pictures that I allowed myself to be in.

When I moved on from my physically demanding job, I finally got a job I always envisioned myself in, an office job. Now it was mentally demanding. At first, I thought I took on more than I could chew, but I adapted. Soon I found myself restless. I was confined. Couldn't interact face to face with others. Once I mastered it, I wasn't happy. I also wasn't happy with the job period, so I moved on.

What I would like to share between my physically demanding job verses my mentally challenging jobs is, mentally challenging jobs are more draining. When I would go home after a long day of walking around all day, my mind was alive and I couldn't sleep at night. When I would go home from my mentally challenging jobs, I couldn't even read a chapter before turning out the lights. I was so mentally exhausted. Even thinking of getting up and going for a walk was too much. Most times, I'm glad when I did, but making myself physically do it was tiresome itself.

You might be wondering, what does weight loss have to do with writing? Well, I'm going to tell you, shortly.

Before COVID-19 took the world by storm, I started incorporating healthier choices into my diet for myself. One of my favorite restaurants, Harvest Seasonal Grill, has many plant-based options. I'm not afraid to try something once, especially when I get tired of the same things over and over again. The restaurant pairs unusual foods that I never thought would go well with each other. Every time I dare to try something outside of my comfort zone, I'm surprised. Got me into experimenting with cooking at home. I'm not a five-star chef and I like my food bland. Too many restaurants put too much salt and flavoring. If I want salty lips, all I have to do is swim in the ocean.

I made gradual changes along the way. Cut down on sweets and salty foods. Cut back on sweets so much that when there were potlucks at work and I sampled one too many sweet treats, I had sugar surges. It's a real thing. Being all jittery. Heart rate racing. Not a good thing. Don't know how I managed to type on the keyboard afterwards.

Even though I made gradual changes and was making healthier choices, the weight wasn't coming off. In fact, I had gained more than ever after I left my once physically demanding job. Got into the same rhythm of sitting all day in a chair and doing nothing when I got home from work except watching television and eating mindlessly. Of course, there were plenty of other things I could be doing, other than daily chores, like writing, but that required more brain cells and no one, character-wise, was speaking loud enough.

When COVID changed the world, I found myself working from home, like many others. Got out of the house less. When I was in the office, I took my breaks and walked. Took my lunch and walked. Now, I wasn't taking those walks. Started to get some knee pain. I refused to allow it to escalate, so I made myself go for an afternoon walk around my neighborhood.

M. C. Ryder

When my working day was done, I made myself go for walks out on the trails, even though they were more populated. I'm a creature of habit and like my alone time, but COVID changed that too. I knew the times to go when it was less crowded, so I didn't have to worry about being run over by bicyclists or joggers. Could slip into my own world and formulate stories that didn't always make it to paper. There's always a story crafting in my mind. Some are louder than others.

To save time, I signed up for a plant-based service, Splendid Spoon, for lunches while working from home. A good way to get some vegetables into my diet, and then made supper. Since I wasn't going out as much, I decided to revisit a story I had started writing, but never finished, *The Darkest Side of the Moon*. I know it's not my best work, it could have been written better, but without it, the rest of the stories would not have emerged.

For two years straight, I worked and wrote non-stop. Grew frustrated when daily life got in the way. I was finally committed. The characters were fresh in my mind. Even stopping to put fuel in my body was a nuisance, but I still had to take care of myself. Lucky for me, I had quick options that were nutritious.

I used to be one who weighed themselves every day. That's toxic to your mentality. I didn't have to see what the scale said to know I put on weight. My clothing told me just fine. Now they were starting to hang loose. So, I took a peek. Watched the weight drop off. Writing wasn't the only thing that changed in my life. A personal matter did as well that caused a great deal of stress, my grandma. Writing helped me to escape. Kept me busy, so I wasn't sitting on the couch eating mindlessly while my cats curled up to take a nap. Transported me away from all the negativity.

I wasn't out in the world, but I was living life through my stories. Trying new things as I did the research and got into the zone. The weight kept shedding. There were times when I would eat, carbs even, and go to bed, wake up, and discover I lost weight. Funny, because all my life I just looked at food, went to bed, and gained weight. Now I was on the opposite spectrum.

You may be asking, what is the moral of this story? Well, I'm going to tell you. I understand now how skinny girls stay skinny and tend to eat what they want.

Stress.

Stress does a funny thing to a person. It can make you or break you. I used to stress eat. Sometimes I'm still guilty of it. Somewhere along the way, stress is what changed my metabolism. Like I mentioned earlier, I changed my eating habits for myself. Cut the majority of processed foods from my diet and focused on healthy, whole foods. I used to be able to eat a whole bag of chips in one sitting. To me now, it's like eating air. Empty calories. Not filling. It never was, that's why I was never satisfied and kept wanting something more, only to never truly be satisfied.

It never registered what I've always heard conveyed. No one can tell you what to do. You have to figure it out for yourself, based on your needs. Everyone is unique. Determination to make a change for yourself is what will make you successful. You know your body better than anyone else, even better than doctors. I don't need an official diagnosis to know I'm overweight.

I've seen so many scenarios in my lifetime where the expression is stated, "that will never happen." Let me tell you, the impossible is always possible. Nothing you read will ever prepare you for when the impossible becomes possible. Too many doctors are sticklers for what is written in the medical books and what they are taught by hearsay. It's not until you find yourself in a scenario you have no or little training in when only in your dreams becomes reality.

Always do your homework. The internet is a double-edge sword. It has great information and exaggerated information. You must always read between the lines. Doctors can't help you if they don't ask the right questions and if you don't know the right questions to ask. Just like your fingerprints, everyone is unique. What works for one person won't necessary work for you.

I'm not naïve, I know part of my weight loss was also due to some depression I experienced. Again, I didn't need a diagnosis to know I was experiencing depression. I was aware of the situation I was in and I refused to allow it to drag me under. I was fortunate enough to write a character who experienced depression, so I knew the signs. I knew how to combat it. I didn't go for medication. I tried reaching out to those close in my circle for some support. I got some, but not as much as I had hoped. I never blamed anyone, as I never told them what I was really going through. They only knew the surface of it.

The hardest thing to go through is watching a family member deteriorate right before your eyes, in your own home while also working from home, unable to do anything about it as there is no cure when death comes knocking on one's door. It's even harder when it's dragged out slowly. Harder yet when that family member has never been nice to you your whole life. When I asked what was one thing my grandma loved about me, and not because we're related by blood, she couldn't answer. Again, silence is an answer. It stung at the time, but later I realized it was because she didn't know how to love herself.

Everyone has something they are going through. A reason why you should *always* be kind to everyone you encounter. Mindful of the comments you say. Think before you speak. If you are thinking about something, chances are they've heard it many times before. You never know if that one innocent and simple comment is the reason for someone to go over the edge.

Chapter Twenty-Seven
New Chapter

During the summer of 2023, not only was I battling waves of depression, I was also battling loneliness. I found myself working from home in a quiet and empty house, with the exception of thunder paws racing around in the morning. I wanted to go back into the office full-time, but the thing stopping me was the fact that hardly anyone was in the office, and the ones that were there well, they didn't talk to me.

My job demanded quantity not quality of the work. It was frowned upon when one was talking to other employees. The environment, toxic. I learned the hard way not to appear too smart, as it only intimidated others. It was so bad in the department I worked in that I jumped at the opportunity to switch to a different department. Picked up on the work quick, and it just didn't challenge me anymore, after a few months.

When an opportunity presented itself, I applied to a different department that paid more, since I had six furry mouths to feed now. I didn't want to leave the positive and welcoming environment, but for my mentality, it was necessary. The new department challenged me for a while, yet the environment was chilled. I stayed away from the unnecessary drama. Had a supervisor who challenged me that the other employees despised.

When COVID-19 entered the picture, I was sent to work from home. In the beginning, I enjoyed it. It was a blessing in disguise when my grandma's health took a turn for the worst in 2022. I was able to juggle working from home, taking care of her, taking care of my six felines, and taking care of the house. When she passed, even though she found peace, the house wasn't the same anymore. My original supervisor retired, and I had a new supervisor who left me alone, which was nice, but I found I wasn't being challenged anymore.

Although the workload was immense for the whole department, the work I was tasked with I could complete in no time. When I don't feel valued or I'm taken advantage of, I don't go the extra mile. I do the bare minimum. In the beginning, I will give 110%, go above and beyond, but when I'm met with silence and don't feel appreciated, I hold back. What ends up happening is I end up punishing myself. I want to help. Want to make a difference. Want to hear that what I do matters. When I don't feel any of that, I question what my purpose is.

When my grandma passed, I ended up throwing myself into my author business. It was, in a sense, a coping mechanism and also gave me purpose where my day job lacked. It was unhealthy to be working two full-time jobs at the same time. When I tried reaching out to others, I grew frustrated, as no one seemed to want to make time for me. To be fair, they had no idea what I was going through. I just wanted to find a way to get out of the house after my day job. Wanted to have something to do socially. I accepted a long time ago that if I wanted to do something, I had to do it myself and I embraced that, but things had changed. Just because I could go to the movie theater by myself, didn't mean that I wanted to now. I loved my nature walks, but I wasn't craving alone time anymore.

My mom worked second shift, so I didn't get to see her often during the weekdays. The days crawled until the weekends. I had the writer's group at my local library, but that was only once a month. I found another place to go to at a different library that talked about bestsellers, but again that was once a month.

Of course, I had writing I could turn to, but I just didn't have the motivation. After I completed The Dark series, I wanted to take a break and recover from burnout. My mind also felt emptier since my characters were no longer occupying space. A first for me. Although there are always stories to be written, a character doesn't talk to me loudly until they are named. That was something else I had to cope with that I didn't see coming. I created this fantasy world that I was sucked into that felt so real, and then I was blasted back into reality. I wanted to go back to my fantasy world where I had control.

I applied to several places both at my current job and outside of the job. I had interviews, but didn't get hired. Other places that I applied to, I heard not a word. There was one outside job I got a phone call, but after playing phone tag shortly after my grandma passed, I decided I was no longer interested. I continued my search all summer long. Found it ironic Taylor Swift's *Cruel Summer* became a single. It was a cruel summer for me.

When Autumn began, I still didn't have luck anywhere I applied. Went back to the one place I thought was the job for me and noticed the position I applied for was still open. I reapplied and waited. After two weeks, I got a call to set up an interview. Went to the interview as my authentic self. I wasn't as nervous as I normally am for an interview. I really had nothing to lose, only to gain. It was about two weeks later when I got the call offering me the position. I didn't hesitate to say yes, even if it was a pay cut. I had to trust that everything would work out. What I knew for certain, I couldn't stay at my current job. It was sucking the life out of me. True, the grass may not be greener on the other side, but I recall writing something along the way that you will never know if you don't try. See, my own words circle back to me.

One thing I learned about myself; I'm not meant for a full-time remote job. When your house becomes a prison, something's wrong. Something needs to change. The only one in control is yourself. Change is scary, but it's absolutely necessary to evolve.

When I emailed my letter of resignation, I didn't know what to expect. All I received back was a thank you and a list of information to complete, so the paperwork could be completed. My supervisor didn't beg or plead for me to stay. Didn't even ask where I was going.

On my last day, it was business as usual. Most people would do the bare minimum and not care since they are half out the door. I was the opposite. I worked harder without holding back and completed all the accounts emailed to me to tackle for the next week, so I could lessen the load for whoever would be assigned my work site. The minimum quantity of work I'm supposed to complete on a daily basis, I doubled.

I got escorted out of the door, early after turning in all company-owned equipment. Went home and once again the house felt emptier. The hardest thing a person can do is to walk away from the known into the unknown. Part of me wanted to run back and tell them I made a mistake, but the way I was treated confirmed I made the right decision. No one should ever go to a place of employment and feel like a robot. Not have social interactions. Not be treated like a human being without feelings. Just because a job pays well or has great benefits, it's not worth your mental health in staying.

Even though I went into a new job knowing what I was getting myself into, I really didn't know until orientation. Became overwhelmed with information overload. Part of me wanted to run away and say this isn't for me after all, but I stuck with it. Not only did I have the determination not to fail or admit to defeat, but something else happened that I didn't expect. I took a job that took in troubled youth to help nurture and provide them a healing environment, and in turn, it was also healing to me. Most traumas I have never experienced, yet there are some mentally I have. To go from a toxic environment to a positive one was beyond heartwarming. I won't lie, I had doubts that I didn't belong and tried to run and find another job shortly after, but destiny had other plans.

My Journey as an Author

So, I embraced the new chapter in my life with high hopes. Hoped it was the place I'm meant to be. Time will tell, of course, but the one thing I know for certain is the positives outweigh the negatives in turning the page and beginning anew.

Chapter Twenty-Eight
The Darkened Enchantment

The Darkened Enchantment had not originally been planned. I wrapped up *All I See Are Dark Clouds* as I envisioned. The trilogy was supposed to end there, but I couldn't help to wonder, what if? I had a new character, Lily. I also had a name, Cleo. I thought it fitting for Lily to be born on the same day as Nadine. To be a Sagittarius, the fire element.

The wheels kept turning. What if I had her grow up to be a firefighter? I knew nothing about firefighting other than the shows I watch on television, but television doesn't show you everything. Like always, research was needed in order for my idea to work. There is a lot of information out there online. Yes, I could have gone to my local fire department, but there were certain things I had to think about. Each state is different, so I had to take that into consideration. Sometimes I don't even know to question certain things until I'm actually writing. I tried my best to make the firefighter element in my story as believable as I could.

When it comes to plants, I am no expert. I know the popular ones. That's about it. I don't have a green thumb. Try to remember to water the plants I do have. They don't always make it. Again, I had to do some research. Had to find what fit with my story and what was native in each state I referenced in my story. Writing is hard. There is a lot of details you have to take into consideration. Even though my story is a work of fiction, I still wanted as much truth as possible. I know I learned a great deal in my journey writing the story. Learned a lot more about plants. Read a book on botany. I'm still no expert, but I have more wisdom from it.

Between the two girls, Cleo is hands down my favorite. There are seeds of myself in all of my female characters, but Cleo is definitely one where a lot of girls can connect with, including myself.

The character that stole my heart in this one was Mutsu. I also loved Saffron and dislike with a passion what was necessary for the story. I had other ideas for her. They didn't happen.

I went into this story with a different approach. I hadn't planned on it and if I didn't complete it, I would have been okay with that. This was just for fun and to see where it would go. Let me tell you, writing a story with two different character narratives is difficult, especially when they are opposite. Some chapters I wrote back-to-back before slipping into the other character's mind. It was easy in the beginning, but when I got to the part when both characters were in the same space as one another, it got harder.

I got frustrated, not knowing what direction to go, before I had the idea to split them apart once more. That helped me, but I still had some difficulties about halfway through the story and I was ready to quit. I took a break and went back to the beginning and reread what I wrote. I try to avoid going back to the beginning because it takes me out of the current head space, but when I did, I knew I couldn't quit. It was strong. I had to give my characters justice and finish the story, somehow. I pushed myself and did just that until I hit another wall.

In my mind, I knew how I wanted the story to end. I just didn't know how to get there.

There was something missing. A big piece of the puzzle that I just couldn't grasp. I decided to go back to my roots. To the character that started it all. Nadine. Her favorite spice was cinnamon. I decided to google all about cinnamon. What I found amazed me. That was the piece of the puzzle I was missing. A crucial piece. Everything I read about cinnamon somehow fit with my story. So, I ran with it. What I managed to create in the end, I think, was just brilliant.

It was just one little piece that was missing that connected the whole story. Not just this story, but the whole series. Sometimes you just have to sit back and wait for that missing piece to reveal itself. It was always there, just overlooked. Never give up. Even in your darkest hour, the sun still rises. Sometimes you just got to look for the sunshine a little harder.

I knew the direction I was going to go with the girls. It was the first time I wrote a story like it. So far, with each of my stories, I was able to include a lot of diverse characters. This was an opportunity to include more diversity. There was an element from *The Darkest Side of the Moon* that I ended up cutting since it didn't fit. I won't lie, I was disappointed. I really wanted it to work, but for the characters, it didn't. I decided it was perfect for this story, so I recycled part of it. Sometimes there is a reason that certain things don't work out for one story, but end up working for another. That was the case for this one. I'm glad I was able to bring it back. It's something that is important and overlooked way too much.

Permission.

Just because someone thinks it's okay and they get a good vibe, doesn't mean it's okay to take what you want. Always ask for permission, especially if you don't know someone too well. Never assume.

It was fun to bring Tommy back. Fun to explore his character and make him completely different from when he was introduced in *The Darkest Side of the Moon*. This story was basically my way of throwing everything in that I could think of from all the prior ones. I was on an epic wild ride just like all of you until I had to tie everything together and make sense of it. Not an easy task.

With each story I wrote, as you know, I added new characters. By the time I got to this one, I really hated myself. There were way too many characters and I couldn't assume my readers read every single book in the series. I had to think of something crafty to get rid of them, without killing them. Ha-ha. I had to remind myself, although I adore many of my characters, this wasn't their story. This story was about Lily and Cleo and how they interacted, at times, with prior characters from the past. Once I got that squared away in my mind, the writing went a little smoother.

Writing my stories back-to-back to back, I believe, made my writing stronger. With each story I completed, I had this sense I wouldn't write anything better and then I surprised myself. *All I See Are Dark Clouds* was my masterpiece, in my mind. This one was just brilliant. Good stories don't have to be long. I don't know which one I like better because they are both great in their unique ways.

Chapter Twenty-Nine
Infinity Tales

I believe, hands down, this was the hardest story to write in my series. I don't like to make promises I can't keep. I don't like to put added pressure on my shoulders. When writing becomes a job and not an enjoyment, I told myself I would stop. Not only did I make a promise to my mom to write a Leo story, but I also wanted to write it, to honor Tiggie.

That was always my intent. Tiggie. He deserved a solo story. The reason this one was so difficult to write was because I had to go back to the beginning. The first few chapters were easy. Leo as a kitten. I wanted to put everything that a cat may go through. This was my chance to not only honor Tiggie, but also every cat in this world. To put you, the reader, through a cat's eyes. I've lived with cats my whole life, so I knew a thing or two about them.

The other problem which made the story difficult to write, was the tone. The very first word that sets the tone for the whole story is *sad*. That wasn't my original intention, but thinking about Leo's life over the course of all the stories, yeah, there was a lot of sadness he went through. That all cats in this world go through. What made it even harder was the fact that I was going through a difficult time in my personal life. When I wrote *All I See Are Dark Clouds,* I didn't truly know what depression felt like. Only grasped the surface of it. Now I was in a dark place, drowning, trying to keep above the current that just kept slamming against me and pushing me under. I was writing this story at the worst time in my life, but I was afraid to stop because I wanted to get it done. I *needed* to get it done. I owed it to my mom. And I owed it to Tiggie.

Once things went south with Nadine's character, it was a whirlwind to write Leo's story. When I wrote my other short stories, I had more freedom or a particular point in time to focus on. With Leo, he was featured in every story, so I had to go back and review every place I mentioned him plus add compelling extras when he wasn't around the main characters. I'm going to be honest, I enjoyed writing those extras more than retelling his side of the story when he was around my main characters. When I finish a story and I finish editing, I'm mentally done with it and want to move on. I don't like to be dragged backwards.

Not everything in Leo's story was gloomy. There were some parts that I thoroughly enjoyed writing. Sparked some humor. The one that comes to mind is the first meeting between Camille and Michael's characters. I really enjoyed writing that part. Without Leo's story, I never would have had a chance to revisit that pivotal moment.

Another section I enjoyed writing was Leo's interaction with Beckett. There was a part in *All I See Are Dark Clouds* that I wrote that may have some critics questioning. I kept it in because it made sense, but in Leo's story, I got to explore how the partnership came about. I still learn more about my characters with each story I write.

The other main reason I knew I needed to write Leo's story was because I had to correct something that happened at the end of *The Darkened Enchantment* that didn't sit well with me, that I came to regret, but it was necessary for the story. This was an opportunity to correct a wrongdoing.

Chapter Thirty
Burnout

Like I mentioned earlier, I've always been a writer. I've had the rollercoaster ride every writer does. From writer's block to self-doubt. It took me over ten years to write *The Darkest Side of the Moon*, but once I finished, I didn't stop there. I continued on. I always knew in my mind I wanted to write three stories.

The short stories along the way were just bonus. Once my spark was lit, I didn't want to stop. I was on fire and everything was there in the raw. I had to get it all out before the flame burned out. I spent two years writing The Dark series back-to-back to back. Plus, I had to live life and an unforeseen circumstance hinged me. Only, I didn't give up. I kept making time, much to my furry friends' protest, because there was magic in each of my stories. Magic, I needed to get out. The problem was, I was overloading my mind. Not only was I still working a full-time job, which was using my mind, I was also transporting myself into these characters in order to tell their stories, which really burned me out. I was exhausted.

Mentally. Every time I had to leave and drive somewhere, I started to become concerned about getting into an accident. My reflexes were not as on point. I also had a personal matter I was going through. Struggled to stay above depression. I'm glad I wrote about depression before I actually experienced it. Depression has two sides. A person can wallow in their self-worth and do nothing about it or a person can find themselves in a situation out of their control, that they are unable to escape from, even when they ask for help. At the end of the day, it's always your choice what to do. Drown in misery or fight the current to rise above. You are always responsible for yourself, first. You can't help anyone who doesn't want to help themselves. Period. All you can do is try your best, but don't put yourself under for them.

I knew what I needed to do, though, for myself. Take a break for starters, soak up some sunshine, and I needed to refuel my mind. I looked up natural foods that did just that. At the top of the list were beets, avocado, walnuts, blueberries, and dark chocolate. It was the end of blueberry season and kept getting some at my local farm market. I already ate dark chocolate, but I was not craving it. Decided to get some beet juice and eat some avocado. I got walnuts, but they are still around waiting to be eaten.

While working on *When Darksome Falls*, I caved and took my break. I reached a point in the story where I wasn't certain I liked the direction it was going. I took about two weeks off writing, however, I wrote about my journey and edited that instead. I wasn't ready to call it quits just yet, just needed a break. Gave more of my time to my furry friends. Visited a friend. Went to lunch with some family I hadn't seen in a long time. It was the break I needed before hitting the keyboard again. Slipping back into my character's mindset. I won't lie. It was a daunting task. The thing about writing my stories back-to-back to back-to-back was that they were all still fresh in my mind. All the characters and their voices. So, it was easy to dive in headfirst to start a new story because the character was already crafted. The world was already crafted.

I made excuses. I procrastinated. Wanted to get back and finish *When Darksome Falls*, but I thought I might have taken too much time away and it wouldn't measure up. Don't get me wrong. The story idea was still there and developed somewhat along the way, but I've done it countless times before. Stopped and never went back to finishing my story. Once I get out of the character's head, it's hard for me to get back into that mindset.

One day, a new YouTube video popped up by Abbie Emmons. I will admit, sometimes being stalked online by my interests is beneficial. In this case, it was. I often times listened to the channel. A lot of what's said is point on. Actually, all of it is. I've learned a lot over my years of reading and writing, but never took the time to process what I learned for myself that was now being expressed into words. What spoke to me was, "the gift is always there." That was exactly what I needed to hear at the right time. That was what gave me the spark to get back to writing and finishing Melia's story.

Moral of the story. If you have a gift, don't be afraid to share it. If people around you don't respect your gift, there are others out there that you don't know about who will. You never know who you touch with your gift by just being yourself. Don't listen to all the negative. That is just noise trying to drown you out. Tune it out. Focus on what makes *you* happy. Touching souls and putting smiles on people's faces is the best feeling in the world. That speaks way more volumes than negative comments.

Chapter Thirty-One
When Darksome Falls

I ended *The Darkened Enchantment* in a way that should have been the end of the series, but the series wasn't done with me. There was still one more story that wanted to be told. I dreaded it. When I wrote *A Dance Between Light and Darkness*, I grew annoyed with Melia's character. It's not her fault. It's just who she was as a person. A good-hearted person who gets taken advantaged of over and over again. All too real because I see it on a daily basis and it frustrates me. I'm also one who gets taken advantaged of with acts of kindness.

I didn't want to have to slip into her head again. Tried to avoid writing the story altogether, but my mind wouldn't stop asking what if? The more I thought, the more outlined in my head. I had to remind myself that Melia grew as a character and was not completely who she was back then. She had changed. She was still sweet and innocent, but she also learned some things along the way in her journey.

The main focus on this story was self-discovery. She came from a dark place. There were still some questions left unanswered. I was able to avoid it then, but now, as the story progressed, I was forced to answer them. Had to dig a little deeper and understand her character. It was easy to develop her in third-person. Now I was writing her story in first-person. Was inside her head. In the beginning, she started off as the same whiny girl I couldn't stand who made foolish decisions. It was necessary, but so hard to write.

However, I knew the place she was in and where she would eventually go. As the dots connected, it just made complete sense. Her character didn't grow too much when she turned into a vampire. She was happy and content with her life with Vince, running away from her past. Now she had to face it. So did I. Funny how you don't see something until you are forced to. It was why she wouldn't let me let go of the series. She had a voice that still wanted to be heard. I was justified in giving it to her.

I'm a fan of *Yellowstone*. I'm not an expert when it comes to cowboys and ranches, but that show left a lasting imprint. I can't recall what exactly lead me to Texas, but when I decided that's where I wanted my story to take place, I saw an opportunity.

I don't know anything about the cattle business. The type of grass they eat. Didn't know there was so many different kinds of grass and not only that, but certain grasses that grow in warmer climate or cooler. I had to do some digging. A lot of it. There is so much information out there that it becomes overwhelming. It was an in over my head moment. Melia's reactions to the information Danny provides was a "you and me both," moment. Of course, I exaggerated the details since it is a work of fiction and I needed it to work for the story I was telling. However, so many times, I thought of calling it quits. I had to remind myself this story takes place in the future and the sky was the limit. Wanted some factual information, but also had the freedom of fictionalizing it. I just needed the right formula.

Another thing I did some digging into was the beef industry. The dark side of it. I had a vague knowledge base, but like most people, I avoided the ugly truth. In order to write something believable, I had to do some research into it. Saw horrific images that scarred my eyes. Read disgusting details that churned my stomach. Read *Mad Cowboy* by Howard F. Lyman. Afterwards, I had to take another break.

Another scene I researched was the process of preparing a chicken for consumption. There are details that did not make it into the story that turned me away from eating chicken. Beef wasn't a problem since I hardly eat it in the first place, but

My Journey as an Author

chicken and fish are my go-to meats. For a period of time, I stopped eating meat altogether. When I did, it had an effect on me. Took me some time to figure it out. What you put into your body has a big impact. What you remove also has an impact.

I came to the realization that no one truly knows where food comes from unless you are managing it yourself. You are trusting and relying on others to source it ethically. You don't know what animals are treated with or what vegetables and fruits are treated with. What I do know is how my body responds to it. When I get fruit from the grocery stores, I can taste the chemicals versus when I get fruit from local farm markets. Bigger isn't always better.

I love horses. As a little girl growing up, during recess at my elementary school, I would often wander off to hang out with the horses that lived at the farm behind the school. There was also a horse, Kirby, in my town that I loved visiting every day. I would hand feed him grass and other treats, but mostly grass. He was always gentle. Brown with a bit of white on his nose. He wasn't an appaloosa though, as the Kirby portrayed in *When Darksome Falls*. I selected the breed for two reasons. The horse's temperament, and it's the favorite breed to a good friend of mine.

I would talk to my Kirby often, and he would whine back. He was the highlight of my day, every day. I was devastated when he passed away. He only exists in my memory because cell phones weren't a thing when I was growing up. I have a poster of a random horse that looks similar, that's all worn and ripped, but it's the closest picture I have of Kirby. He was my friend and to this day, I still remember him, always. He imprinted a hoof-print on my heart and was one in a million. Now I had an opportunity to pay tribute to him.

Unfortunately, today, I have to be careful around horses as I've developed allergies to them. It's funny how I never had a problem when I was around Kirby, but once I wasn't around him on a daily basis, now I break out into hives if I touch them. So heartbreaking because I still love horses.

While I was in the middle of writing *When Darksome Falls*, I was also in the process of getting *A Dance Between Light and Darkness* published. When it came time that I received my formatted manuscript to review and edit, I was hesitant. Worried I would lose the spark in writing Melia from a Melia who was young and innocent. I had to try to keep the two separated. The good news, it only fueled my creative spark. Allowed me to see the parallels of her character from who she was then to who she was now.

When I reached the scene when she has a conversation with the Pastor, that took a great deal of time to write. I wanted to capture the right words and the right message. I had to review many quotes of different subjects to get what was brewing in the back of my mind out, and into my own words, that made sense. Had to stop and process before I could sail forward.

I was not aware of how I subconsciously reverted Melia back to who she was before she found happiness with Vince. She never truly knew herself back then. Never had an opportunity to find out what she was made of. When it clicked, I was ready to write the end. A storm was brewing, and I knew it was going to be intense. I started off not wanting to continue Melia's story, but in the end, she redeems herself and it was electrifying how it all came full circle.

Chapter Thirty-Two
The Holy Spirit

I'm not one who likes to get too personal. Some things are not meant to be advertised, but I think it's important to include a chapter because I'm certain I'm not the only one who struggles with faith. I didn't even like voicing my opinion to my own mother because I didn't want to disappoint her. Disliked when I get questioned about my faith. I wanted to believe wholeheartedly, but I always had reservations to protect myself from disappointment. Have even wondered if the Bible is the biggest scam of all. I have not read it in entirety, yet. It's a big undertaking. I've gone to church, but there has always been misdoubt in the people who preach about one thing, and I found to do the opposite. Don't like being forced to do something because that's the norm.

What I like about church are the inspiring messages. There's always something I can take away, but I never liked the spotlight. On my writing journey, I had to dig deep. Writing has always been my therapy and gave me a voice when I found I didn't have one. Even if no one ever read it, it allowed me to get out what I buried inside. Trust doesn't come easy for me. There is always someone who wants to use you against yourself for their benefit. That is why I've learned to be guarded.

Although I did not have a close relationship with God before I wrote The Dark series, I cannot deny that I've grown closer to Him during my journey writing the series. So many times, I would reread what I wrote and think to myself, *I wrote that?* I would also wonder, *where did that come from?*

I always shied away, even bringing Him up in anything, but He was a big part in the stories. The one story I'm most proud of is *The Path to Redemption* in *A Darker Demise*. I never set out on writing about suicide and the aftermath of it. As I was writing it, it opened my eyes. Made me question, what truly happens after? I don't have the answer, but I'd like to believe in what was accomplished in my story. Redemption.

These stories I've managed to craft weren't just from me. He might not have spoken to me directly, but He spoke to me through my fingers. Spoke to me by providing the right quotes and information that I researched in order to capture the right words to convey the stories. When I thought about giving up, He provided subtle signs to rekindle that fire burning inside. He gave me the tools before I found myself in my own dark hour. I was meant to write these stories not just for everyone to enjoy, but also for myself.

Sacrifices are necessary. Spiritual ones. It doesn't matter who you believe the Holy Spirit to be. The most important thing is to simply believe. You don't have to go to church every Sunday in order to have faith. The relationship between your God and you is solely *your* business. A sacrifice should never entail a life. That's the Devil's work. A false God. Never follow blindly. Always question everything.

I am blessed that He gifted me and chose me to depict bullying, standing up for oneself, suicide, forgiveness, salvation, redemption, depression, remembrance, true happiness, hope, sacrifice, self-discovery, and even faith. The key ingredient that allows the seeds to sprout from them all, is love. It is *always* love.

Chapter Thirty-Three
The Clowder

The clowder. My furry friends. A story in itself. I took on the role of foster mom, which was supposed to be ten days. My mother's coworker had a stray where he lived that gave birth to the litter. Took them in and wanted to do the right thing, but in order for the SPCA of Lancaster to take them, they needed some human socialization. Unfortunately, he had plans that took him out of state for that duration. I was at a low point in my life, just living day by day, trying to figure out my next move. So, when the opportunity to foster some kittens presented itself, I jumped on board. It was only for ten days, right? Oh, how wrong I was.

I'm a strong person. My mother, on the other hand, is a sucker for a cute face. I should have known better.

When I picked up the little darlings, they were all huddled in the back of the cage, terrified. Not only had they been taken from their mother, but now handed off to a different human. At the time, I had two older cats, Tiggie and Salem. They were independent, however they despised each other so they had to remain separated from each other, at all times. I tried to let them work out their problems, but the problem was me. Salem was a stray that I took in. At that time, we had another cat, Fluffy. I got lucky. After Salem was quarantined in my room for a period of time, and was gradually introduced to Fluffy, they became best friends. Tiggie, on the other hand, not so much luck. When my great-grandmother passed, no one was knocking down the door to take him in. He was already an older cat, so he had a lot against him. I knew it was going to be a problem with Salem. I took the same steps, quarantined Tiggie in my room before introducing him to the other two. Fluffy didn't care. He was older and a diabetic, so Tiggie didn't try anything with him.

Salem, on the other hand, was a different story. Tiggie liked to antagonize him, and he was capable of holding his own. He was an outside cat for a while before being strictly indoors.

The reason I said I'm the problem is because I brought in a new family member and cast Salem out of my room. A room he grew to learn he could come to as he pleased once the door was left wide open, but now was suddenly closed. I bonded with Salem before I took him in. I can only imagine he felt like I was trying to replace him. I wasn't, but cats are stubborn. I do believe their rift was more of a territorial thing over me.

When we moved, I was hopeful that neutral ground would help alleviate the problem, but it didn't. They had to remain separated at all times and I had to split my time between them. My relationship with Salem also shifted. He was angry at me all the time and let me know it.

I got into a rhythm with the two. I wasn't happy about it. In order to keep the peace, I wasn't left with much choice. Enter the bundles of joy. I seriously don't know what I was thinking at the time because I had to keep them separated from the adults. However, I was committed and it was only supposed to last ten days. It was a boost to my spirit.

The way to anyone's heart is food. So, I filled up the food dishes, when they were present, so they could hear, before I opened the cage door, found a place a distance away, and waited. At the time, I didn't know who they were as individuals. I can only assume, but I don't know for sure since there were four solid black cats, that Monkey was the one that was the first to step outside of the cage and helped himself to grub.

Monkey. Oh, Monkey. He is a goofball. The special one and the most curious. Gets him into trouble, a lot. It's his curiosity of the world that gives the others confidence. He was the first one I could touch. The first one that came to me. The first one who bonded with me in a way no other cat has before. When I was down at his level, he liked to climb on my back. Loves to play, with any and everything. Even something so simple as a straw. Don't lay it on the counter and expect it to be there when you get back. He's a thief! Hence the name Monkey. He's also a very demanding child. Has a treat obsession and lets you know it when treat-time is late. He's also a mini dog who likes to bring toys back to me, that I tossed for him. Never taught him that. He did that all on his own. If only I could put him in a harness and take him for a walk. Nope. Does not like anything on him. Got him a monkey costume for Halloween and he just rolls and rolls to try and get it off.

His brother, basically his twin and hard to tell apart, was the second to come to me and bond. I dubbed him Smudge. A temporary name only to be able to associate them from each other. Like Monkey, he was all black, with the exception of a little spot on his back paw that looked like a smudge. Hence the name.

Never take in strays during kitten season because they will never leave. You will be stuck with them for life. Even when you try to ask coworkers and friends, when you show pictures and they think they are adorable, the problem is a lot of people already have pets and can't take on more. Lucky for me, I was able to find a loving home for one, Smudge, who was renamed Ocho. Even though I loved him dearly, I'm so glad he got out of the mix. Right away I saw a jealous thing between him and Monkey. Again, I was the problem. It was over my attention.

It took the others more time to warm up to me. Monkey was the one that paved the path. When they realized I wasn't so scary after all, they became comfortable around me. Playtime was their favorite time and, of course, feeding time. It was mine too. I couldn't wait to get home from work. Although, they were smart ones and gave me a run for my money. I cornered them off from spaces I didn't want them to get into, but they found a way anyway. Every time I tried to outsmart them, they undermined me.

I gave temporary names to all of them in the beginning. Gray, now Jade, Runt, now Raven, Spot, now Spottie, and Lion, now Luna. Luna was a hisser in the beginning. The protector of her siblings. The problem was, it wasn't that scary of a hiss because she was still finding her voice. It was adorable. Think Simba from *The Lion King*.

Raven is my little princess. She knows it and plays the part well. Has this sweet little meow. I had a particular fondness for her because she was the smallest of the litter.

Jade, as her temporary name conveys, is all gray. I've always wanted a gray cat and now I have one. She is one with attitude. A queen. Let's me know when it's time to fill the dry. She loves to eat. I'm always having to tell her to stop eating everyone else's portion of wet before they get a fair chance.

The love brothers, as I like to refer to them. Spottie, a blend of black and white, who I wanted to name Yin Yang originally, but got overruled, and Fuzzy, the only long-haired one. They love snuggling up together and Fuzzy is always in Spottie's shadow. I can tell Spottie gets annoyed at times, but he still loves him. When it's treat-time, they love butting their heads against each other.

Treat-time. The sound of thundering paws. One shake is definitely all it takes and watch out. You will be run over. They have an obsession, and if they don't get their treats when they are supposed to, Fuzzy will howl his head off. Monkey will cry the blues. Your life will be miserable until you give them what they want. There is no bargaining. Little monsters. Frankly, I don't know how I managed to get any writing done in my house. I had to put myself first, and they did not like it. I socialized them alright. Too much! They all fight over my lap when I actually sit down on the couch or chair. If they would allow me to multitask, I would give them more time, but when I sit it's all about them. Pet me. Pet me.

Pet me. Mom, get off your phone. Mom, stop reading. Mom, stop trying to eat a hot meal.

I know better than to say, "never say never," but I'm okay with never, ever having human children. Furry children are quite enough. I can sympathize with what every mother in this world goes through. I know what it's like to want five minutes alone in the bathroom, and your child barges through the door because they don't like closed doors. To say they are a handful is being nice.

Don't get me wrong. I'm good around children. I spent a decade of my life around young children. They are smarter than many give them credit. I just don't have any interests in having my own, unless the right person comes along to change my mind. Seen too many people have them for all the wrong reasons. It's a life commitment with too many of them abandoned and feeling unwanted. And then you wonder why the world is the way it is?

Chapter Thirty-Four
Final Thoughts

If you're trying to be somebody to prove something to someone else, then you're going to fail because that is for all the wrong reasons. If you're trying to be somebody to prove something to yourself, then you're going to succeed because you're doing it for the right reasons.

I'm going to let you in on a little secret, no one's going to believe in you as much as you believe in yourself.

In your journey, you'll have some supporters, but you'll also come across as being intimidating. The only time anyone outside of your circle will ever truly see you is when you make something of yourself. Then they will want to be your best friend. Surround yourself with those that lift you up, not tear you down. I promise, you are better off without them. Listen to your gut instinct. If you don't feel comfortable around certain individuals, then they are not the right people for you. They want to see you fail not rise above or they want to profit off of *your* success. If being yourself is not enough for them, move on. It's their loss, not yours. You don't need them in your life. Don't be afraid to stray.

Don't be afraid to go off the beaten path. You are unique. Be an inspiration. Follow your dreams and don't let anyone tell you that you can't. They just want to get in your head and see you fail. The mind is a powerful thing. You can do anything you want as long as *you* believe *you* can achieve it. There's a reason there are more skeptics than believers. Climb that mountain. Don't let it deter you. As long as you are putting one step in front of the other, you are doing more than you were before. Don't do anything for the wrong reasons, do it for the greater good. The best leaders are the ones that decide *not* to follow the crowd. There have only ever been a few who saw my potential while everyone else underestimated me. Being underestimated only fueled my fire. I was never one to be afraid to think outside of the box.

Allow me to introduce the bitter truth. No one is entitled to anything. No fortune, no fame, no followers. You have to earn everything through hard work. If you are allergic to hard work, everything you have can just as easily be taken away. It's only a disguise.

When I started writing my series, I had not planned on the theme that connected them all to be between love and hate, but that's where they went. It was more than good and evil. Right and wrong. Vampires and werewolves. What started out as fanfiction blossomed into something beautiful and powerful. It even moved me. Even to this day, I'm still in disbelief I was able to write something so insightful. I accomplished my mission even if I don't become a viral sensation. At the end of the day, I want to inspire others and teach through my writing and experiences.

I'm not here to please everyone. If you want to write a bad review and speak negative about my novels, that's your prerogative. Just know you missed the big picture in my stories. I feel sorry for you. And news flash, some people, me included, will go out of their way to do the opposite of something negative said. I make my own assessments. I never take one individual's opinion at face value.

I am only one person. I have to remind myself that every day because I do try to do it all, but sometimes it's impossible and exhausting. Hence the editing mistakes that are still found in my novels. Sometimes the universe is against me, even when I try my hardest to make them perfect. How many times have I said I'm not? Know this, I'm still finding my way and navigating off the beaten path of my journey. Thank you for joining me.

Afterword

I started writing about my journey during my first year as an author and talked about many ups and downs. A lot of labor of love went into trying to make my mark in the world, and I'm still trying as I've found it's not easy. Writing was only the beginning. Even though I may not be exactly where I had hoped to be, I have been blessed with many opportunities. When DE MODE magazine reached out to me to be featured in their magazine, I never imagined they would reach out again during year two and ask me to be on the cover of their magazine. It was an opportunity not to pass on, even though I was still trying to recover financially from releasing books back-to-back and spending more than I intended my first year.

I'm not one who typically likes pictures of myself. I avoid the camera like the plague, but becoming an author, I had to change. It's part of my job now. I had to get comfortable in putting my image out there. If I was going to be a face on a magazine, I had to do it right and get some professional ones. I had a tight deadline to get everything done. Knowing how hard I worked as a small business, I wanted to give another small business an opportunity. It just so happened that I knew a photographer who has been supportive of my author journey. Now it was an opportunity to give back. And so, I called up Jen from JK Photography, LLC and asked if she could fit me in and she did! I was stiff at first, but she got me to open up and did great work. I actually liked seeing pictures of myself.

Change can be a scary thing, but oftentimes it's necessary. We, as humans, are creatures of habit. I mentioned about

My Journey as an Author

starting a new chapter at a new job and unfortunately it didn't work out for me, but everything happens for a reason. I was able to heal from my past trauma just by taking the job in trying to help others. I also made a new, supportive friend. In desperation to leave the job, I accepted a job at a place I never thought I would end up. Was conflicted, but it ended up being the place I needed to be where I could still help others by just being myself. Although there is drama, I choose to be happy. Choose to be positive every day instead of bitter. It's a breath of fresh air when I can just be myself and be accepted as is. To inspire a group of individuals down in life with hope that dreams can come true if you work hard enough, and reach for what you want. It's easy to dream about where you might see yourself in five years, but it's hard to pave the path to achieve that dream. Self-doubt will always be there to bring you down to your knees, but it's always a choice to listen to the noise or block it out.

If I'm not comfortable with just an image of myself, I'm even more terrified of being on camera. However, I knew that appearing on ABC27 Good Day PA was a local advertising opportunity, that would only cost me my time, to be on the show. I gathered the courage to fill out the form and arranged a date. Told my coworkers how nervous I was as the day got closer, but they all believed in me. Believed I would do great. Helped me to almost believe it myself.

On the big day, I got taken to the green room with the others who would also be on the show, promoting their business or organization. I wasn't the only newbie. Got to meet Josh from Solarity Energy Solutions and made a new friend/fan. When it was his turn to go on air, he nailed it. When my turn came, the nerves were still there and showed a bit, but I got through it! I faced my fears of the camera in my face, three to be exact, and got through it without stuttering too much.

I interviewed with Brett Thackara who was very nice, and helped calm my nerves. He even encouraged me to come back when releasing my next book in The Dark series. At the time, it had not even crossed my mind to go back, however the day was so uplifting with such positivity from everyone that works in the studio, that it was definitely on my mind now. I even got to shake Amy Kehm's hand, when meeting her in person! The thing is, even though I may see the hosts on television all the time, they are humans too. They are just ordinary people with a job in the spotlight, along with the people behind the cameras. I got to see how they all work together. My cat clone of Tiggie was an ice-breaker, and everyone thought he was a real cat.

I wrote it once and I'll write it again. I'm still navigating my journey as an author. It's a journey I'll be on for the rest of my life. Opportunities tend to come when I least expect them, often when I'm feeling down. However, I don't stay down for long. At the end of the day, it's about my stories. About reaching people with my stories. Helping people with my stories. My stories are my way of giving back. Changing lives. Inspiring.

SNEAK PEEK FEATURE FROM

The Ride of Your Life

M. C. Ryder

Part One
Fun Summer Job

Prologue

There's a hiss-like sound as the brakes disengage and the train rolls forward down a slight descent barely noticed when standing on the platform.

Thud-thud, thud-thud, thud-thud, the train makes as it leaves the station and becomes hard to hear once it completely leaves. Soon a clink-clack is heard as the train reaches the chain-lift, connecting onto it, and clank, clank, clanks up the whole way.

Right now, it's easy to hear with no crowd lined up waiting to ride. The only individuals in the station are new hires along with ride trainers. No other loud noises fill the station since the amusement park is not open to the public. It's training day for the new hires going into a new summer season. All are shy and nervous. For most, this is their first job ever. A lot of the employees are either still in high school or in college. Most of the gene pool are teenagers, but there is a mix of middle age and elderly.

There's a moment of silence as the train crests the top before a whoosh is heard! The train drops down from the highest drop and gains the speed it needs, up to 50 mph, to course its way along the track. It snakes through all the turns, rushing near the station soon to be far away again. The whoosh sound goes right by the queuing ramp and the cracking of wood as it bares the weight of the train. A completely normal occurrence as the wooden track is not made to be stiff, as it needs to be able to shift with the weight of the train and the occupants. All one needs to do is focus and pay close attention to any wooden roller coaster and one can see the track shift when the train rushes by. An amazing sight to see.

The train speeds around the last turn and as it crests the slight hill, several flashes go off all at once, simultaneously, as the camera takes pictures of each set of seats.

Irk-irk, irk-irk, the train makes as it slows down by the set of brakes before reaching the back of the station.

The train stops automatically on the back brake due to the second train still sitting in the station. Once the back of the 2nd train passes the sensor, right outside of the station, the 1st train advances forward. The brakes all work together at the appropriate time, clamping shut and re-opening, as the 1st train slowly purrs forward into the station. Once the front part of the train is lined up with the sensor, all the brakes clamp shut and a slight release of air can be heard. The long black bar sitting in the middle of the track, automatically rises by air pressure to release the lap bars of the train.

One by one, each newbie takes their turn operating and dispatching the trains out of the station and getting the necessary hands-on experience needed to run such a large piece of machinery. However, learning how the ride runs is only step one. No ride operator can be fully prepared for unusual situations, that arise on a daily basis during the heat of the summer season. The only way to learn how to handle peculiar situations is by experiencing them for oneself. It's easy to learn how to operate a ride and become used to the repetitive routine, but once the park is open and guests are thrown into the mix, the experience changes dramatically.

Once everyone confirms with the trainers that they all feel confident in operating The Ferocious Cat, the appropriate paperwork is filled out and they move onto the next ride.

SNEAK PEEK FEATURE FROM

Heart & Soul Lyrics
(Volume 1)

M. C. Ryder

As I Am
(November 26, 2023)

Got stuck on repeat
Lost who I wanted to be
While playing a game
I was never going to win

Got lost on a lonely road
Called out to anyone
Who might be listening
But no one lent a helping hand

I've reached the edge
I've had enough
It's time to be more than I am

So, love me or hate me
Take me as I am
No longer am I going to
Keep on people-pleasing
When I don't need approval
I'm just going to be me
So, take me as I am

Got buried in the sand
As time slipped away
Wasting precious minutes
That I'll never regain

Got sick of being disregarded
When I know that I'm
Someone that's worthy

Of being respected

I won't step over the edge
I'm going to stand tall
And start being more than I am

So, love me or hate me
Take me as I am
No longer am I going to
Keep on people-pleasing
When I don't need approval
I'm just going to be me
So, take me as I am

It's never enough
Anything I do
You can't buy love
Since it'll never be true

So, love me or hate me
Take me as I am
No longer am I going to
Keep on people-pleasing
When I don't need approval
I'm just going to be me
So, take me as I am

Got to stay loyal
To the spirit within
So, love me or hate me
Take me as I am

Courtesy of JK Photography, LLC

About the Author

M. C. Ryder has been composing stories, poems, and lyrics from the beginning of time when reading became a learned trait. The sky is the limit but enjoys exploring off the beaten path both figuratively and literally. Resides in the Keystone State with a clowder of felines who rule the house. Enjoys long trail walks during the cozy tinge of Autumn, appreciates music with deep lyrical meaning, and relishes in reading a variety of genres.

Website: https://www.mcryderauthor.com

- M. C. Ryder (page)
- MCRyder0
- mcryder0
- mcryder0
- mcryder0

www.ingramcontent.com/pod-product-compliance
Lightning Source LLC
Chambersburg PA
CBHW020500030426
42337CB00011B/172